The Fugitive Blacksmith

The Fugitive Blacksmith:
Or, Events in the History of James W. C. Pennington,
Pastor of a Presbyterian Church, New York, Formerly a Slave in the State of Maryland, United States

James W. C. Pennington

©1849.

The Fugitive Blacksmith

THE FUGITIVE BLACKSMITH;
OR,
EVENTS IN THE HISTORY OF JAMES W. C. PENNINGTON, PASTOR OF A PRESBYTERIAN CHURCH, NEW YORK, FORMERLY A SLAVE IN THE STATE OF MARYLAND, UNITED STATES.

"Let mine outcasts dwell with thee, Moab; be thou a covert to them from the face of the spoiler.--ISAIAH xvi. 4.

Second Edition

1849.

MR. CHARLES GILPIN,

MY DEAR SIR,

    The information just communicated to me by you, that another edition of my little book, "The Fugitive Blacksmith," is called for, has agreeably surprised me. The British public has laid me under renewed obligations by this mark of liberality, which I hasten to acknowledge. I would avail myself of this moment also, to acknowledge the kindness of the gentlemen of the newspaper press for the many favourable reviews which my little book has received. It is to them I am indebted, in no small degree, for the success with which I have been favoured in getting the book before the notice of the public.

Yours truly,

J. W. C. PENNINGTON.

Hoxton, Oct. 15th, 1849.

The Fugitive Blacksmith

PREFACE.

THE brief narrative I here introduce to the public, consists of outline notes originally thrown together to guide my memory when lecturing on this part of the subject of slavery. This will account for its style, and will also show that the work is not full.

The question may be asked, Why I have published anything so long after my escape from slavery? I answer I have been induced to do so on account of the increasing disposition to overlook the fact, that THE SIN of slavery lies in the chattel principle, or relation. Especially have I felt anxious to save professing Christians, and my brethren in the ministry, from falling into a great mistake. My feelings are always outraged when I hear them speak of "kind masters,"--"Christian masters,"--"the mildest form of slavery,"--"well fed and clothed slaves," as extenuations of slavery; I am satisfied they either mean to pervert the truth, or they do not know what they say. The being of slavery, its soul and body, lives and moves in the chattel principle, the property principle, the bill of sale principle; the cart-whip, starvation, and nakedness, are its inevitable consequences to a greater or less extent, warring with the dispositions of men.

There lies a skein of silk upon a lady's work-table. How smooth and handsome are the threads. But while that lady goes out to make a call, a party of children enter the apartment, and in amusing themselves, tangle the skein of silk, and now who can untangle it? The relation between master and slave is even as delicate as a skein of silk: it is liable to be entangled at any moment.

The mildest form of slavery, if there be such a form, looking at the chattel principle as the definition of slavery, is comparatively the worst form. For it not only keeps the slave in the most unpleasant apprehension, like a prisoner in chains awaiting his trial; but it actually, in a great majority of cases, where kind masters do exist, trains him under the most favourable circumstances the system admits of, and then plunges him into the worst of which it is capable.

It is under the mildest form of slavery, as it exists in Maryland, Virginia, and Kentucky, that the finest specimens of coloured females are reared. There are no mothers who rear, and educate in the natural graces, finer daughters than the Ethiopian women, who have the least chance to give scope to their maternal affections. But what is generally the fate of such female slaves? When they are not raised for the express purpose of supplying the market of a class of economical Louisian and Mississippi gentlemen, who do not wish to incur the expense of rearing legitimate families, they are, nevertheless, on account of their attractions, exposed to the most shameful degradation, by the young masters in the families where it is claimed they are so well off. My master once owned a beautiful girl about twenty-four. She had been raised in a family where her mother was a great favourite. She was her mother's darling child. Her master was a lawyer of eminent abilities and great fame, but owing to habits of intemperance, he failed in business, and my master purchased this girl for a nurse. After he had owned her about a year, one of his sons became attached to her, for no honourable purposes; a fact which was not only well-known among all of the slaves, but which became a source of unhappiness to his mother and sisters.

The result was, that poor Rachel had to be sold to "Georgia." Never shall I forget the heart-rending scene, when one day one of the men was ordered to get "the one-horse cart ready to go into town;" Rachel, with her few articles of clothing, was placed in it, and taken into the very town where her parents lived, and there sold to the traders before their weeping eyes. That same son who had degraded her, and who was the cause of her being sold, acted as salesman, and bill of saleman. While this cruel business was being transacted, my master stood aside, and the girl's father, a pious member and exhorter in the Methodist Church, a venerable grey-headed man, with his hat off, besought that he might be allowed to get some one in the place to purchase his child. But no; my master was invincible. His reply was, "She has offended in my family, and I can only restore confidence by sending her out of hearing." After lying in prison a short time, her new owner took her with others to the far South, where her parents heard no more of her.

Here was a girl born and reared under the mildest form of slavery. Her original master was reputed to be even indulgent. He lived in a town, and was a high-bred gentleman, and a lawyer. He had but a few slaves, and had no occasion for an overseer, those negro leeches, to watch and drive them; but when he became embarrassed by his own folly, the chattel principle doomed this girl to be sold at the same sale with his books, house, and horses. With my master she found herself under far more stringent discipline than she had been accustomed to, and finally degraded, and sold where her condition could not be worse, and where she had not the least hope of ever bettering it.

This case presents the legitimate working of the great chattel principle. It is no accidental result--it is the fruit of the tree. You cannot constitute slavery without the chattel principle--and with the chattel principle you cannot save it from these results. Talk not then about kind and christian masters. They are not masters of the system. The system is master of them; and the slaves are their vassals.

These storms rise on the bosom of the calmed waters of the system. You are a slave, a being in whom another owns property. Then you may rise with his pride, but remember the day is at hand when you must also fall with his folly. To-day you may be pampered by his meekness; but to-morrow you will suffer in the storm of his passions.

In the month of September, 1848, there appeared in my study, one morning, in New York City, an aged coloured man of tall and slender form. I saw depicted on his countenance anxiety bordering on despair, still I was confident that he was a man whose mind was accustomed to faith. When I learned that he was a native of my own state, Maryland, having been born in the county of Montgomery, I at once became much interested in him. He had been sent to me by my friend, William Harned, Esq., of the Anti-Slavery Office, 61, John Street. He put into my hand the following bill of distress:--

"Alexander, Virginia, *September 5th, 1848.*

"The bearer, Paul Edmondson, is the father of two girls, Mary Jane and Emily Catherine Edmondson. These girls have been purchased by us, and once sent to the South; and upon the positive assurance that the money for them would be raised if they were brought back, they were returned. Nothing, it appears, has as yet been done in this respect by those who promised, and we are on the very eve of sending them south a second time; and we are candid in saying, that if they go again, we will not regard any promises made in relation to them.

"The father wishes to raise money to pay for them, and intends to appeal to the liberality of the humane and the good to aid him, and has requested us to state in writing *the conditions upon which we will sell his daughters.*

"We expect to start our servants to the South in a few days; if the sum of twelve hundred dollars be raised and paid us in fifteen days, or we be assured of that sum, then we will retain them for twenty-five days more, to give an opportunity for raising the other thousand and fifty dollars, otherwise we shall be compelled to send them along with our other servants.

(Signed) "BRUIN AND HILL."

The old man also showed me letters from other individuals, and one from the Rev. Matthew A. Turner, pastor of Asbury Chapel, where himself and his daughters were members. He was himself free, but his wife was a slave. Those two daughters were two out of fifteen children he had raised for the owner of his wife. These two girls had been sold, along with four brothers, to the traders, for an attempt to escape to the North, and gain their freedom.

On the next Sabbath evening, I threw the case before my people, and the first fifty dollars of the sum was raised to restore the old man his daughters. Subsequently the case was taken up under the management of a committee of ministers of the Methodist Episcopal Church, consisting of the Rev. G. Peck, D.D., Rev. E. E. Griswold, and Rev. D. Curry, and the entire sum of 2,250 dollars, (£450.) was raised for two girls, fourteen and sixteen years of age!

But why this enormous sum for two mere children? Ah, reader, they were reared under the mildest form of slavery known to the laws of Maryland! The mother is an invalid, and allowed to live with her free husband; but she is a woman of excellent mind, and has bestowed great pains upon her daughters. If you would know, then, why these girls were held at such a price; even to their own father, read the following extract of a letter from one who was actively engaged in behalf of them, and who had several interviews with the traders to induce them to reduce the price, but without success. Writing from Washington, D. C., September 12th, 1848, this gentleman says to William Harned, "The truth is, *and is confessed to be, that their destination is prostitution;* of this you would be satisfied on seeing them: they are of elegant form, and fine faces."

And such, dear reader, is the sad fate of hundreds of my young countrywomen, natives of my native state. Such is the fate of many who are not only reared under the mildest form of slavery, but of those who have been made acquainted with the milder system of the Prince of Peace.

When Christians, and Christian ministers, then, talk about the "mildest form of slavery,"--"Christian masters," &c., I say my feelings are outraged. It is a great mistake to offer these as an extenuation of the system. It is calculated to mislead the public mind. The opinion seems to prevail, that the negro, after having toiled as a slave for centuries to enrich his white brother, to lay the foundation of his proud institutions, after having been sunk as low as slavery can sink him, needs now only a second-rate civilization, a lower standard of civil and religious privileges than the whites claim for themselves.

During the last year or two, we have heard of nothing but revolutions, and the enlargements of the eras of freedom, on both sides of the Atlantic. Our white brethren everywhere are reaching out their hands to grasp more freedom. In the place of absolute monarchies they have limited monarchies, and in the place of limited monarchies they have republics: so tenacious are they of their own liberties.

But when we speak of slavery, and complain of the wrong it is doing us, and ask to have the yoke removed, we are told, "O, you must not be impatient, you must not create undue excitement. You are not so badly off, for many of your masters are kind Christian masters." Yes, sirs, many of our masters are professed Christians; and what advantage is that to us? The grey heads of our fathers are brought down by scores to the grave in sorrow, on account of their young and tender sons, who are sold to the far South, where they have to toil without requite to supply the world's market with *cotton, sugar, rice, tobacco, &c.* Our venerable mothers are borne down with poignant grief at the fate of their children. Our sisters, if not by the law, are by common consent made the prey of vile men, who can bid the highest.

In all the bright achievements we have obtained in the great work of emancipation, if we have not settled the fact that the chattel principle is wrong, and cannot be maintained upon Christian ground, then we have wrought and triumphed to little purpose and we shall have to do our first work over again.

It is this that has done all the mischief connected with slavery; it is this that threatens still further mischief. Whatever may be the ill or favoured condition of the slave in the matter of mere personal treatment, it is the chattel relation that robs him of his manhood, and transfers his ownership in himself to another. It is this that transfers the proprietorship of his wife and children to another. It is this that throws his family history into utter confusion, and leaves him without a single record to which he may appeal in vindication of his character, or honour. And has a man no sense of honour because he was born a slave? Has he no need of character?

Suppose insult, reproach, or slander, should render it necessary for him to appeal to the history of his family in vindication of his character, where will he find that history? He goes to his native state, to his native county, to his native town; but no where does he find any record of himself *as a man.* On looking at the family record of his old, kind, Christian, master, there he finds his name on a catalogue with the horses, cows, hogs and dogs. However humiliating and degrading it may be to his feelings to find his name written down among the beasts of the field, *that* is just the place, and the *only* place assigned to it by the chattel relation. I beg our Anglo-Saxon brethren to accustom themselves to think that we need something more than mere kindness. We ask for justice, truth and honour as other men do.

My coloured brethren are now widely awake to the degradation which they suffer in having property vested in their persons, and they are also conscious of [illegible] he deep and corrupting disgrace of having our wives and children owned by other men--men, who have shown to the world that their own virtue is not infallible, and who have given us no flattering encouragement to entrust that of our wives and daughters to them.

I have great pleasure in stating that may dear friend W. W., spoken of in this narrative, to whom I am so deeply indebted, is still living. I have been twice to see him within four years, and have regular correspondence with him. In one of the last letters I had from him, he authorises me to use his name in connection with this narrative in these words,--"As for using my name, by reference or otherwise, in thy narrative, it is at thy service. I know thee so well James, that I am not afraid of thy making a bad use of it, nor am I afraid or ashamed to have it known that I took thee in and gave thee aid, when I found thee travelling alone and in want.--W. W."

On the second page of the same sheet I have a few lines from his excellent lady, in which she says, "James, I hope thee will not attribute my long silence in writing to indifference. No such feeling can ever exist towards thee in our family. Thy name is mentioned almost every day. Each of the children claims the next letter from thee. It will be for thee to decide which shall have it.--P. W."

In a postscript following this, W. W. says again:--

"Understand me, James, that thee is at full liberty to use my name in any way thee wishes in thy narrative. We have a man here from the eastern shore of thy state. He is trying to learn as fast as thee did when here.--W. W."

I hope the reader will pardon me for introducing these extracts. My only apology is, the high gratification I feel in knowing that this family has not only been greatly prospered in health and happiness, but that I am upon the most intimate and pleasant terms with all its members, and that they all still feel a deep and cordial interest in my welfare.

There is another distinguished individual whose sympathy has proved very gratifying to me in my situation--I mean that true friend of the negro, *Gerrit Smith, Esq.* I was well acquainted with the family in which Mr. Smith married in Maryland. My attention has been fixed upon him for the last ten years, for I have felt confident that God had set him apart for some great good to the negro. In a letter dated Peterborough, November 7th, 1848, he says:--

"J. W. C. PENNINGTON,

"Slight as is my *personal* acquaintance with you, I nevertheless am well acquainted with you. I am familiar with many passages in your history--all that part of your history extending from the time when, a sturdy blacksmith, you were running away from Maryland oppression, down to the present, when you are the successor of my lamented friend, Theodore S. Wright. Let me add that my acquaintance with you inspired me with a high regard for your wisdom and integrity."

Give us a few more such men in America, and slavery will soon be numbered among the things that [illegible] ere. A few men who will not only have the moral courage to aim the severing blow at the chattel relation between master and slave, without parley, palliation or compromise; but who have also the christian [illegible] delity to brave public scorn and contumely, to seize [illegible] coloured man by the hand, and elevate him to the position from whence the avarice and oppression of [illegible] whites have degraded him. These men have the [illegible] view of the subject. They see that in every [illegible] where the relation between master and slave is broken, slavery is weakened, and that every coloured [illegible] elevated, becomes a step in the ladder upon which his whole people are to ascend. They would not have us accept of some modified form of liberty, while the old mischief working chattel relation remains unbroken, untouched and unabrogated.

J. W. C. PENNINGTON.

13, *Princes Square, London,*
August 15*th*, 1849.

CONTENTS.
CHAPTER I.

- My birth and parentage--The treatment of Slaves generally in Maryland . . . . .

CHAPTER II.

- The flight . . . . .

CHAPTER III.

- A dreary night in the woods--Critical situation the next day . . . . .

CHAPTER IV.

- The good woman of the toll-gate directs me to W. W.--My cordial reception by him . . . . .

CHAPTER V.

- Seven months' residence in the family of J. K., a member of the Society of Friends in Chester County, Pennsylvania--Removal to New York--Becomes a convert to religion--Becomes a teacher . . . . .

CHAPTER VI.

- Some account of the family I left in slavery--Proposal to purchase myself and parents--How met by my old master . . . . .

CHAPTER VII.

- ○ The feeding, clothing, and religious instruction of the slaves in the part of Maryland where I lived . . . . .
- APPENDIX . . . . .

THE FUGITIVE BLACKSMITH.

CHAPTER I.

MY BIRTH AND PARENTAGE.--THE TREATMENT OF SLAVES GENERALLY IN MARYLAND.

I WAS born in the state of Maryland, which is one of the smallest and most northern of the slave-holding states; the products of this state are wheat, rye, Indian corn, tobacco, with some hemp, flax, &c. By looking at the map, it will be seen that Maryland, like Virginia her neighbour, is divided by the Chesapeake Bay into eastern and western shores. My birthplace was on the eastern shore, where there are seven or eight small counties; the farms are small, and tobacco is mostly raised.

At an early period in the history of Maryland, her lands began to be exhausted by the bad cultivation peculiar to slave states; and hence she soon commenced the business of breeding slaves for the more southern states. This has given an enormity to slavery, in Maryland, differing from that which attaches to the system in Louisiana, and equalled by none of the kind, except Virginia and Kentucky, and not by either of these in extent.

My parents did not both belong to the same owner: my father belonged to a man named ----; my mother belonged to a man named ----. This not only made me a slave, but made me the slave of him to whom my mother belonged; as the primary law of slavery is, that the child shall follow the condition of the mother.

When I was about four years of age, my mother, an older brother and myself, were given to a son of my master, who had studied for the medical profession, but who had now married wealthy, and was about to settle as a wheat planter in Washington County, on the western shore. This began the first of our family troubles that I knew anything about, as it occasioned a separation between my mother and the only two children she then had, and my father, to a distance of about two hundred miles. But this separation did not continue long; my father being a valuable slave, my master was glad to purchase him.

About this time, I began to feel another evil of slavery--I mean the want of parental care and attention. My parents were not able to give any attention to their children during the day. I often suffered much from *hunger* and other similar causes. To estimate the sad state of a slave child, you must look at it as a helpless human being thrown upon the world without the benefit of its natural guardians. It is thrown into the world without a social circle to flee to for hope, shelter, comfort, or instruction. The social circle, with all its heaven-ordained blessings, is of the utmost importance to the *tender child;* but of this, the slave child, however tender and delicate, is robbed.

There is another source of evil to slave children, which I cannot forbear to mention here, as one which early embittered my life,--I mean the tyranny of the master's children. My master had two sons, about the ages and sizes of my older brother and myself. We were not only required to recognise these young sirs as our young masters, but *they* felt themselves to be such; and, in consequence of this feeling, they sought to treat us with the same air of authority that their father did the older slaves.

Another evil of slavery that I felt severely about this time, was the tyranny and abuse of the overseers. These men seem to look with an evil eye upon children. I was once visiting a menagerie, and being struck with the fact, that the lion was comparatively indifferent to every one around his cage, while he eyed with peculiar keenness a little boy I had; the keeper informed me that such was always the case Such is true of those human beings in the slave states, called overseers. They seem to take pleasure in torturing the children of slaves, long before they are large enough to be put at the hoe, and consequently under the whip.

We had an overseer, named Blackstone; he was an extremely cruel man to the working hands. He always carried a long hickory whip, a kind of pole. He kept three or four of these in order, that he might not at any time be without one.

I once found one of these hickories lying in the yard, and supposing that he had thrown it away, I picked it up, and boy-like, was using it for a horse; he came along from the field, and seeing me with it, fell upon me with the one he then had in his hand, and flogged me most cruelly. From that, I lived in constant dread of that man; and he would show how much he delighted in cruelty by chasing me from my play with threats and imprecations. I have lain for hours in a wood, or behind a fence, to hide from his eye.

At this time my days were extremely dreary. When I was nine years of age, myself and my brother were hired out from home; my brother was placed with a pump-maker, and I was placed with a stone mason. We were both in a town some six miles from home. As the men with whom we lived were not slaveholders, we enjoyed some relief from the peculiar evils of slavery. Each of us lived in a family where there was no other negro.

The slaveholders in that state often hire the children of their slaves out to non-slaveholders, not only because they save themselves the expense of taking care of them, but in this way they get among their slaves useful trades. They put a bright slave-boy with a tradesman, until he gets such a knowledge of the trade as to be able to do his own work, and then he takes him home. I remained with the stonemason until I was eleven years of age: at this time I was taken home. This was another serious period in my childhood; I was separated from my older brother, to whom I was much attached; he continued at his place, and not only learned the trade to great perfection, but finally became the property of the man with whom he lived, so that our separation was permanent, as we never lived nearer after, than six miles. My master owned an excellent blacksmith, who had obtained his trade in the way I have mentioned above. When I returned home at the age of eleven, I was set about assisting to do the mason-work of a new smith's shop. This being done, I was placed at the business, which I soon learned, so as to be called a "first-rate blacksmith." I continued to work at this business for nine years, or until I was twenty-one, with the exception of the last seven months.

In the spring of 1828, my master sold me to a Methodist man, named ----, for the sum of seven hundred dollars. It soon proved that he had not work enough to keep me employed as a smith, and he offered me for sale again. On hearing of this, my old master re-purchased. me, and proposed to me to undertake the carpentering business. I had been working at this trade six months with a white workman, who was building a large barn when I left. I will now relate the abuses which occasioned me to fly.

Three or four of our farm hands had their wives and families on other plantations. In such cases, it is the custom in Maryland to allow the men to go on Saturday evening to see their families, stay over the Sabbath, and return on Monday morning, not later than "half-an-hour by sun." To overstay their time is a grave fault, for which, especially at busy seasons, they are punished.

One Monday morning, two of these men had not been so fortunate as to get home at the required time: one of them was an uncle of mine. Besides these, two young men who had no families, and for whom no such provision of time was made, having gone somewhere to spend the Sabbath, were absent. My master was greatly irritated, and had resolved to have, as he said, "a general whipping-match among them."

Preparatory to this, he had a rope in his pocket, and a cowhide in his hand, walking about the premises, and speaking to every one he met in a very insolent manner, and finding fault with some without just cause. My father, among other numerous and responsible duties, discharged that of shepherd to a large and valuable flock of Merino sheep. This morning he was engaged in the tenderest of a shepherd's duties;--a little lamb, not able to go alone, lost its mother; he was feeding it by hand. He had been keeping it in the house for several days. As he stooped over it in the yard, with a vessel of new milk he had obtained, with which to feed it, my master came along, and without the least provocation, began by asking, "Bazil, have you fed the flock?"

"Yes, sir."
"Were you away yesterday?"
"No, sir."
"Do you know why these boys have not got home this morning yet?"

"No, sir, I have not seen any of them since Saturday night."

"By the Eternal, I'll make them know their hour. The fact is, I have too many of you; my people are getting to be the most careless, lazy, and worthless in the country."

"Master," said my father, "I am always at my post; Monday morning never finds me off the plantation."

"Hush, Bazil! I shall have to sell some of you; and then the rest will have enough to do; I have not work enough to keep you all tightly employed; I have too many of you."

All this was said in an angry, threatening, and exceedingly insulting tone. My father was a high-spirited man, and feeling deeply the insult, replied to the last expression,--"If I am one too many, sir, give me a chance to get a purchaser, and I am willing to be sold when it may suit you."

"Bazil, I told you to hush!" and suiting the action to the word, he drew forth the "cowhide" from under his arm, fell upon him with most savage cruelty, and inflicted fifteen or twenty severe stripes with all his strength, over his shoulders and the small of his back. As he raised himself upon his toes, and gave the last stripe, he said, "By the * * * I will make you know that I am master of your tongue as well as of your time!"

Being a tradesman, and just at that time getting my breakfast, I was near enough to hear the insolent words that were spoken to my father, and to hear, see, and even count the savage stripes inflicted upon him.

Let me ask any one of Anglo-Saxon blood and spirit, how would you expect a *son* to feel at such a sight?

This act created an open rupture with our family--each member felt the deep insult that had been inflicted upon our head; the spirit of the whole family was roused; we talked of it in our nightly gatherings, and showed it in our daily melancholy aspect. The oppressor saw this, and with the heartlessness that was in perfect keeping with the first insult, commenced a series of tauntings, threatenings, and insinuations, with a view to crush the spirit of the whole family.

Although it was sometime after this event before I took the decisive step, yet in my mind and spirit, I never was a *Slave* after it.

Whenever I thought of the great contrast between my father's employment on that memorable Monday morning, (feeding the little lamb,) and the barbarous conduct of my master, I could not help cordially despising the proud abuser of my sire; and I believe he discovered it, for he seemed to have diligently sought an occasion against me. Many incidents occurred to convince me of this, too tedious to mention; but there is one I will mention, because it will serve to show the state of feeling that existed between us, and how it served to widen the already open breach.

I was one day shoeing a horse in the shop yard. I had been stooping for some time under the weight of the horse, which was large, and was very tired; meanwhile, my master had taken his position on a little hill just in front of me, and stood leaning back on his cane, with his hat drawn over his eyes. I put down the horse's foot, and straightened myself up to rest a moment, and without knowing that he was there, my eye caught his. This threw him into a panic of rage; he would have it that I was watching him. "What are you rolling your white eyes at me for, you lazy rascal?" He came down upon me with his cane, and laid on over my shoulders, arms, and legs, about a dozen severe blows, so that my limbs and flesh were sore for several weeks; and then after several other offensive epithets, left me.

This affair my mother saw from her cottage, which was near; I being one of the oldest sons of my parents, our family was now mortified to the lowest degree. I had always aimed to be trustworthy; and feeling a high degree of mechanical pride, I had aimed to do my work with dispatch and skill, my blacksmith's pride and taste was one thing that had reconciled me so long to remain a slave. I sought to distinguish myself in the finer branches of the business by invention and finish; I frequently tried my hand at making guns and pistols, putting blades in penknives, making fancy hammers, hatchets, sword-canes, &c., &c. Besides I used to assist my father at night in making straw-hats and willow-baskets, by which means we supplied our family with little articles of food, clothing and luxury, which slaves in the mildest form of the system never get from the master; but after this, I found that my mechanic's pleasure and pride were gone. I thought of nothing but the family disgrace under which we were smarting, and how to get out of it.

Perhaps I may as well extend this note a little. The reader will observe that I have not said much about my master's cruel treatment; I have aimed rather to shew the cruelties incident to the system. I have no disposition to attempt to convict him of having been one of the most cruel masters--that would not be true--his prevailing temper was kind, but he was a perpetualist. He was opposed to emancipation; thought free negroes a great nuisance, and was, as respects discipline, a thorough slaveholder. He would not tolerate a look or a word from a slave like insubordination. He would suppress it at once, and at any risk. When he thought it necessary to secure unqualified obedience, he would strike a slave with any weapon, flog him on the bare back, and sell. And this was the kind of discipline he also empowered his overseers and sons to use.

I have seen children go from our plantations to join the chained-gang on its way from Washington to Louisiana; and I have seen men and women flogged--I have seen the overseers strike a man with a hayfork--nay more, men have been maimed by shooting! Some dispute arose one morning between the overseer and one of the farm hands, when the former made at the slave with a hickory club; the slave taking to his heels, started for the woods; as he was crossing the yard, the overseer turned, snatched his gun which was near, and fired at the flying slave, lodging several shots in the calf of one leg. The poor fellow continued his flight, and got into the woods; but he was in so much pain that he was compelled to come out in the evening, and give himself up to his master, thinking he would not allow him to be punished [illegible] he had been shot. He was locked up that night; the next morning the overseer was allowed to tie him up and flog him; his master then took his instruments and picked the shot out of his leg, and told him, it served him just right.

My master had a deeply pious and exemplary slave, an elderly man, who one day had a misunderstanding with the overseer, when the latter attempted to flog him. He fled to the woods; it was noon; at evening he came home orderly. The next morning, my master, taking one of his sons with him, a rope and cowhide in his hand, led the poor old man away into the stable; tied him up, and ordered the son to lay on thirty-nine lashes, which he did, making the keen end of the cowhide lap around and strike him in the tenderest part of his side, till the blood sped out, as if a lance had been used.

While my master's son was thus engaged, the sufferer's little daughter, a child six years of age, stood at the door, weeping in agony for the fate of her father. I heard the old man articulating in a low tone of voice; I listened at the intervals between the stripes, and lo! he was praying!

When the last lash was laid on, he was let down; and leaving him to put on his clothes, they passed out of the door, and drove the man's weeping child away! I was mending a hinge to one of the barn doors; I saw and heard what I have stated. Six months after, this same man's eldest daughter, a girl fifteen years old, was sold to slave-traders, where he never saw her more.

This poor slave and his wife were both Methodists, so was the wife of the young master who flogged him. My old master was an Episcopalian.

These are only a few of the instances which came under my own notice during my childhood and youth on our plantations; as to those which occurred on other plantations in the neighbourhood, I could state any number.

I have stated that my master was watching the movements of our family very closely. Sometime after the difficulties began, we found that he also had a confidential slave assisting him in the business. This wretched fellow, who was nearly white, and of Irish descent, informed our master of the movements of each member of the family by day and by night, and on Sundays. This stirred the spirit of my mother, who spoke to our fellow-slave, and told him he ought to be ashamed to be engaged in such low business.

Master hearing of this, called my father, mother, and myself before him, and accused us of an attempt to resist and intimidate his "confidential servant." Finding that only my mother had spoken to him, he swore that if she ever spoke another word to him, he would flog her.

I knew my mother's spirit and my master's temper as well. Our social state was now perfectly intolerable. We were on the eve of a general fracas. This last scene occurred on Tuesday; and on Saturday evening following, without counsel or advice from any one, I determined to fly.

CHAPTER II.

THE FLIGHT.

IT was the Sabbath: the holy day which God in his infinite wisdom gave for the rest of both man and beast. In the state of Maryland, the slaves generally have the Sabbath, except in those districts where the evil weed, tobacco, is cultivated; and then, when it is the season for setting the plant, they are liable to be robbed of this only rest.

It was in the month of November, somewhat past the middle of the month. It was a bright day, and all was quiet. Most of the slaves were resting about their quarters; others had leave to visit their friends on other plantations, and were absent. The evening previous I had arranged my little bundle of clothing, and had secreted it at some distance from the house. I had spent most of the forenoon in my workshop engaged in deep and solemn thought.

It is impossible for me now to recollect all the perplexing thoughts that passed through my mind during that forenoon; it was a day of heartaching to me. But I distinctly remember the two great difficulties that stood in the way of my flight: I had a father and mother whom I dearly loved,--I had also six sisters and four brothers on the plantation. The question was, shall I hide my purpose from them? moreover, how will my flight affect them when I am gone? Will they not be suspected? Will not the whole family be sold off as a disaffected family, as is generally the case when one of its members flies? But a still more trying question was, how can I expect to succeed, I have no knowledge of distance or direction. I know that Pennsylvania is a free state, but I know not where its soil begins, or where that of Maryland ends? Indeed, at this time there was no safety in Pennsylvania, New Jersey, or New York, for a fugitive, except in lurking-places, or under the care of judicious friends, who could be entrusted not only with liberty, but also with life itself.

With such difficulties before my mind, the day had rapidly worn away; and it was just past noon. One of my perplexing questions I had settled--I had resolved to let no one into my secret; but the other difficulty was now to be met. It was to be met without the least knowledge of its magnitude, except by imagination. Yet of one thing there could be no mistake, that the consequences of a failure would be most serious. Within my recollection no one had attempted to escape from my master; but I had many cases in my mind's eye, of slaves of other planters who had failed, and who had been made examples of the most cruel treatment, by flogging and selling to the far South, where they were never to see their friends more. I was not without serious apprehension that such would be my fate. The bare possibility was impressively solemn; but the hour was now come, and the man must act and be free, or remain a slave for ever. How the impression came to be upon my mind I cannot tell; but there was a strange and horrifying belief, that if I did not meet the crisis that day, I should be self-doomed--that my ear would be nailed to the door-post for ever. The emotions of that moment I cannot fully depict. Hope, fear, dread, terror, love, sorrow, and deep melancholy were mingled in my mind together; my mental state was one of most painful distraction. When I looked at my numerous family--a beloved father and mother, eleven brothers and sisters, &c.; but when I looked at slavery as such; when I looked at it in its mildest form, with all its annoyances; and above all, when I remembered that one of the chief annoyances of slavery, in the most mild form, is the liability of being at any moment sold into the worst form; it seemed that no consideration, not even that of life itself, could tempt me to give up the thought of flight. And then when I considered the difficulties of the way--the reward that would be offered--the human blood-hounds that would be set upon my track--the weariness--the hunger--the gloomy thought, of not only losing all one's friends in one day, but of having to seek and to make new friends in a strange world. But, as I have said, the hour was come, and the man must act, or for ever be a slave.

It was now two o'clock. I stepped into the quarter; there was a strange and melancholy silence mingled with the destitution that was apparent in every part of the house. The only morsel I could see in the shape of food, was a piece of Indian flour bread, it might be half-a-pound in weight. This I placed in my pocket, and giving a last look at the aspect of the house, and at a few small children who were playing at the door, I sallied forth thoughtfully and melancholy, and after crossing the barn-yard, a few moments' walk brought me to a small cave, near the mouth of which lay a pile of stones, and into which I had deposited my clothes. From this, my course lay through thick and heavy woods and back lands to--town, where my brother lived. This town was six miles distance. It was now near three o'clock, but my object was neither to be seen on the road, or to approach the town by daylight, as I was well-known there, and as any intelligence of my having been seen there would at once put the pursuers on my track. This first six miles of my flight, I not only travelled very slowly, therefore, so as to avoid carrying any daylight to this town; but during this walk another very perplexing question was agitating my mind. Shall I call on my brother as I pass through, and shew him what I am about? My brother was older than I, we were much attached; I had been in the habit of looking to him for counsel.

I entered the town about dark, resolved, all things in view, *not* to shew myself to my brother. Having passed through the town without being recognised, I now found myself under cover of night, a solitary wanderer from home and friends; my only guide was the *north star,* by this I knew my general course northward, but at what point I should strike Penn, or when and where I should find a friend, I knew not. Another feeling now occupied my mind,--I felt like a mariner who has gotten his ship outside of the harbour and has spread his sails to the breeze. The cargo is on board--the ship is cleared--and the voyage I must make; besides, this being my first night, almost every thing will depend upon my clearing the coast before the day dawns. In order to do this my flight must be rapid. I therefore set forth in sorrowful earnest, only now and then I was cheered by the *wild* hope, that I should somewhere and at sometime be free.

The night was fine for the season, and passed on with little interruption for want of strength, until, about three o'clock in the morning, I began to feel the chilling effects of the dew.

At this moment, gloom and melancholy again spread through my whole soul. The prospect of utter destitution which threatened me was more than I could bear, and my heart began to melt. What substance is there in a piece of dry Indian bread; what nourishment is there in it to warm the nerves of one already chilled to the heart? Will this afford a sufficient sustenance after the toil of the night? But while these thoughts were agitating my mind, the day dawned upon me, in the midst of an open extent of country, where the only shelter I could find, without risking my travel by daylight, was a corn shock, but a few hundred yards from the road, and here I must pass my first day out. The day was an unhappy one; my hiding-place was extremely precarious. I had to sit in a squatting position the whole day, without the least chance to rest. But, besides this, my scanty pittance did not afford me that nourishment which my hard night's travel needed. Night came again to my relief, and I sallied forth to pursue my journey. By this time, not a crumb of my crust remained, and I was hungry and began to feel the desperation of distress.

As I travelled I felt my strength failing and my spirits wavered; my mind was in a deep and melancholy dream. It was cloudy; I could not see my star, and had serious misgivings about my course.

In this way the night passed away, and just at the dawn of day I found a few sour apples, and took my shelter under the arch of a small bridge that crossed the road. Here I passed the second day in ambush.

This day would have been more pleasant than the previous, but the sour apples, and a draught of cold water, had produced anything but a favourable effect; indeed, I suffered most of the day with severe symptoms of cramp. The day passed away again without any further incident, and as I set out at nightfall, I felt quite satisfied that I could not pass another twenty-four hours without nourishment. I made but little progress during the night, and often sat down, and slept frequently fifteen or twenty minutes. At the dawn of the third day I continued my travel. As I had found my way to a public turnpike road during the night, I came very early in the morning to a toll-gate, where the only person I saw, was a lad about twelve years of age. I inquired of him where the road led to. He informed me it led to Baltimore. I asked him the distance, he said it was eighteen miles.

This intelligence was perfectly astounding to me. My master lived eighty miles from Baltimore. I was now sixty-two miles from home. That distance in the right direction, would have placed me several miles across Mason and Dixon's line, but I was evidently yet in the state of Maryland.

I ventured to ask the lad at the gate another question-- Which is the best way to Philadelphia? Said he, you can take a road which turns off about half-a-mile below this, and goes to Getsburgh, or you can go on to Baltimore and take the packet.

I made no reply, but my thought was, that I was as near Baltimore and Baltimore-packets as would answer my purpose.

In a few moments I came to the road to which the lad had referred, and felt some relief when I had gotten out of that great public highway, "The National Turnpike," which I found it to be.

When I had walked a mile on this road, and when it had now gotten to be about nine o'clock, I met a young man with a load of hay. He drew up his horses, and addressed me in a very kind tone, when the following dialogue took place between us.

"Are you travelling any distance, my friend?"

"I am on my way to Philadelphia."

"Are you free?"

"Yes, sir."

"I suppose, then, you are provided with free papers?"

"No, sir. I have no papers."

"Well, my friend, you should not travel on this road: you will be taken up before you have gone three miles. There are men living on this road who are constantly on the look-out for your people; and it is seldom that one escapes them who attempts to pass by day."

He then very kindly gave me advice where to turn off the road at a certain point, and how to find my way to a certain house, where I would meet with an old gentleman who would further advise me whether I had better remain till night, or go on.

I left this interesting young man; and such was my surprise and chagrin at the thought of having so widely missed my way, and my alarm at being in such a dangerous position, that in ten minutes I had so far forgotten his directions as to deem it unwise to attempt to follow them, lest I should miss my way, and get into evil hands.

I, however, left the road, and went into a small piece of wood, but not finding a sufficient hiding-place,

and it being a busy part of the day, when persons were at work about the fields, I thought I should excite less suspicion by keeping in the road, so I returned to the road; but the events of the next few moments proved that I committed a serious mistake.

I went about a mile, making in all two miles from the spot where I met my young friend, and about five miles from the toll-gate to which I have referred, and I found myself at the twenty-four miles' stone from Baltimore. It was now about ten o'clock in the forenoon; my strength was greatly exhausted by reason of the want of suitable food; but the excitement that was then going on in my mind, left me little time to think of my *need* of food. Under ordinary circumstances as a traveller, I should have been glad to see the "Tavern," which was near the mile-stone; but as the case stood with me, I deemed it a dangerous place to pass, much less to stop at. I was therefore passing it as quietly and as rapidly as possible, when from the lot just opposite the house, or sign-post, I heard a coarse stern voice cry, "Halloo!"

I turned my face to the left, the direction from which the voice came, and observed that it proceeded from a man who was digging potatoes. I answered him politely; when the following occurred:--

"Who do *you* belong to?"
"I am free, sir."
"Have you got papers?"
"No, sir."
"Well, you must stop here."
By this time he had got astride the fence, making his way into the road. I said,
"My business is onward, sir, and I do not wish to stop."
"I will see then if you don't stop, you black rascal."

He was now in the middle of the road, making after me in a brisk walk.

I saw that a crisis was at hand; I had no weapons of any kind, not even a pocket-knife; but I asked myself, shall I surrender without a struggle. The instinctive answer was "No." What will you do? continue to walk; if he runs after you, run; get him as far from the house as you can, then turn suddenly and smite him on the knee with a stone; that will render him, at least, unable to pursue you.

This was a desperate scheme, but I could think of no other, and my habits as a blacksmith had given my eye and hand such mechanical skill, that I felt quite sure that if I could only get a stone in my hand, and have time to wield it, I should not miss his knee-pan.

He began to breathe short. He was evidently vexed because I did not halt, and I felt more and more provoked at the idea of being thus pursued by a man to whom I had not done the least injury. I had just began to glance my eye about for a stone to grasp, when he made a tiger-like leap at me. This of course brought us to running. At this moment he yelled out "Jake Shouster!" and at the next moment the door of a small house standing to the left was opened, and out jumped a shoemaker girded up in his leather apron, with his knife in hand. He sprang forward and seized me by the collar, while the other seized my arms behind. I was now in the grasp of two men, either of whom were larger bodied than myself, and one of whom was armed with a dangerous weapon.

Standing in the door of the shoemaker's shop, was a third man; and in the potatoe lot I had passed, was still a fourth man. Thus surrounded by superior physical force, the fortune of the day it seemed to me was gone.

My heart melted away, I sunk resistlessly into the hands of my captors, who dragged me immediately into the tavern which was near. I ask my reader to go in with me, and see how the case goes.

The Fugitive Blacksmith

GREAT MORAL DILEMMA.

A few moments after I was taken into the bar-room, the news having gone as by electricity, the house and yard were crowded with gossippers, who had left their business to come and see "the runaway nigger." This hastily assembled congregation consisted of men, women, and children, each one had a look to give at, and a word to say about, the "nigger."

But among the whole, there stood one whose name I have never known, but who evidently wore the garb of a man whose profession bound him to speak for the dumb, but he, standing head and shoulders above all that were round about, spoke the first hard sentence against me. Said he, "That fellow is a runaway I know; put him in jail a few days, and you will soon hear where he came from." And then fixing a fiend-like gaze upon me, he continued, "if I lived on this road, *you* fellows would not find such clear running as you do, I'd trap more of you."

But now comes the pinch of the case, the case of conscience to me even at this moment. Emboldened by the cruel speech just recited, my captors enclosed me, and said, "Come now, this matter may easily be settled without you going to jail; who do you belong to, and where did you come from?"

The facts here demanded were in my breast. I knew according to the law of slavery, who I belonged to and where I came from, and I must now do one of there things-- I must refuse to speak at all, or I must communicate the fact, or I must tell an untruth. How would an untutored slave, who had never heard of such a writer as Archdeacon Paley, be likely to act in such a dilemma? The first point decided, was, the facts in this case are my private property. These men have no more right to them than a highway robber has to my purse. What will be the consequence if I put them in possession of the facts. In forty-eight hours, I shall have received perhaps one hundred lashes, and be on my way to the Louisiana cotton fields. Of what service will it be to them. They will get a paltry sum of two hundred dollars. Is not my liberty worth more to me than two hundred dollars are to them?

    I resolved therefore, to insist that I was free. This not being satisfactory without other evidence, they tied my hands and set out, and went to a magistrate who lived about half a mile distant. It so happened, that when we arrived at his house he was not at home. This was to them a disappointment, but to me it was a relief; but I soon learned by their conversation, that there was still another magistrate in the neighbourhood, and that they would go to him. In about twenty minutes, and after climbing fences and jumping ditches, we, captors and captive, stood before his door, but it was after the same manner as before--he was not at home. By this time the day had worn away to one or two o'clock, and my captors evidently began to feel somewhat impatient of the loss of time. We were about a mile and a quarter from the tavern. As we set out on our return, they began to parley. Finding it was difficult for me to get over fences with my hands tied, they untied me, and said, "New John," that being the name they had given me, "if you have run away from any one, it would be much better for you to tell us!" but I continued to affirm that I was free. I knew, however, that my situation was very critical, owing to the shortness of the distance I must be from home: my advertisement might overtake me at any moment.

On our way back to the tavern, we passed through a small skirt of wood, where I resolved to make an effort to escape again. One of my captors was walking on either side of me; I made a sudden turn, with my left arm sweeping the legs of one of my captors from under him; I left him nearly standing on his head, and took to my heels. As soon as they could recover they both took after me. We had to mount a fence. This I did most successfully, and making across an open field towards another wood; one of my captors being a long-logged man, was in advance of the other, and consequently nearing me. We had a hill to rise, and during the ascent he gained on me. Once more I thought of self-defence. I am trying to escape peaceably, but this man is determined that I shall not.

My case was now desperate; and I took this desperate thought: "I will run him a little farther from his coadjutor; I will then suddenly catch a stone, and wound him in the breast." This was my fixed purpose, and I had arrived near the point on the top of the hill, where I expected to do the act, when to my surprise and dismay, I saw the other side of the hill was not only all ploughed up, but we came suddenly upon a man ploughing, who as suddenly left his plough and cut off my flight, by seizing me by the collar, when at the same moment my pursuer seized my arms behind. Here I was again in a sad fix. By this time the other pursuer had come up; I was most savagely thrown down on the ploughed ground with my face downward, the ploughman placed his knee upon my shoulders, one of my captors put his upon my legs, while the other tied my arms behind me. I was then dragged up, and marched off with kicks, punches and imprecations.

We got to the tavern at three o'clock. Here they again cooled down, and made an appeal to me to make a disclosure. I saw that my attempt to escape strengthened their belief that I was a fugitive. I said to them, "If you will not put me in jail, I will now tell you where I am from." They promised. "Well," said I, "a few weeks ago, I was sold from the eastern shore to a slave-trader, who had a large gang, and set out for Georgia, but when he got to a town in Virginia, he was taken sick, and died with the small-pox. Several of his gang also died with it, so that the people in the town became alarmed, and did not wish the gang to remain among them. No one claimed us, or wished to have anything to do with us; I left the rest, and thought I would go somewhere and get work."

When I said this, it was evidently believed by those who were present, and notwithstanding the unkind feeling that had existed, there was a murmur of approbation. At the same time I perceived that a panic began to seize some, at the idea that I was one of a small-pox gang. Several who had clustered near me, moved off to a respectful distance. One or two left the bar-room, and murmured, "better let the small-pox nigger go."

I was then asked what was the name of the slave-trader. Without premeditation, I said, "John Henderson."

"John Henderson!" said one of my captors, "I knew him; I took up a yaller boy for him about two years ago, and got fifty dollars. He passed out with a gang about that time, and the boy ran away from him at Frederickstown. What kind of a man was he?"

At a venture, I gave a description of him. "Yes," said he, "that is the man." By this time, all the gossippers had cleared the coast; our friend, "Jake Shouster," had also gone back to his bench to finish his custom work, after having "lost nearly the whole day, trotting about with a nigger tied," as I heard his wife say as she called him home to his dinner. I was now left alone with the man who first called to me in the morning. In a sober manner, he made this proposal to me: "John, I have a brother living in Risterstown, four miles off, who keeps a tavern; I think you had better go and live with him, till we see what will turn up. He wants an ostler." I at once assented to this. "Well," said he, "take something to eat, and I will go with you."

Although I had so completely frustrated their designs for the moment, I knew that it would by no means answer for me to go into that town, where there were prisons, handbills, newspapers, and travellers. My intention was, to start with him, but not to enter the town alive.

I sat down to eat; it was Wednesday, four o'clock, and this was the first regular meal I had since Sunday morning. This over, we set out, and to my surprise, he proposed to walk. We had gone about a mile and a half, and were approaching a wood through which the road passed with a bend. I fixed upon that as the spot where I would either free myself from this man, or die in his arms. I had resolved upon a plan of operation--it was this: to stop short, face about, and commence action; and neither ask or give quarters, until I was free or dead!

We had got within six rods of the spot, when a gentleman turned the corner, meeting us on horse-back. He came up, and entered into conversation with my captor, both of them speaking in Dutch, so that I knew not what they said. After a few moments, this gentleman addressed himself to me in English, and I then learned that he was one of the magistrates on whom we had called in the morning; I felt that another crisis was at hand. Using his saddle as his bench, he put on an extremely stern and magisterial-like face, holding up his horse not unlike a field-marshal in the act of reviewing troops, and carried me through a most rigid examination in reference to the statement I had made. I repeated carefully all I had said; at the close, he said, "Well, you had better stay among us a few months, until we see what is to be done with you." It was then agreed that we should go back to the tavern, and there settle upon some further plan. When we arrived at the tavern, the magistrate alighted from his horse, and went into the bar-room. He took another close glance at me, and went over some points of the former examination. He seemed quite satisfied of the correctness of my statement, and made the following proposition: that I should go and live with him for a short time, stating that he had a few acres of corn and potatoes to get in, and that he would give me twenty-five cents per day. I most cheerfully assented to this proposal. It was also agreed that I should remain at the tavern with my captor that night, and that he would accompany me in the morning. This part of the arrangement I did not like, but of course I could not say so. Things being thus arranged, the magistrate mounted his horse, and went on his way home.

It had been cloudy and rainy during the afternoon, but the western sky having partially cleared at this moment, I perceived that it was near the setting of the sun.

My captor had left his hired man most of the day to dig potatoes alone; but the waggon being now loaded, it being time to convey the potatoes into the barn, and the horses being all ready for that purpose, he was obliged to go into the potatoe field and give assistance.

I should say here, that his wife had been driven away by the small-pox panic about three o'clock, and had not yet returned; this left no one in the house, but a boy, about nine years of age.

The Fugitive Blacksmith

As he went out, he spoke to the boy in Dutch, which I supposed, from the little fellow's conduct, to be instructions to watch me closely, which he certainly did.

The potatoe lot was across the public road, directly in front of the house; at the back of the house, and about 300 yards distant, there was a thick wood. The circumstances of the case would not allow me to think for one moment of remaining there for the night--the time had come for another effort--but there were two serious difficulties. One was, that I must either deceive or dispatch this boy who is watching me with intense vigilance. I am glad to say, that the latter did not for a moment seriously enter my mind. To deceive him effectually, I left my coat and went to the back door, from which my course would be direct to the wood. When I got to the door, I found that the barn, to which the waggon must soon come, lay just to the right, and overlooking the path I must take to the wood. In front of me lay a garden surrounded by a picket fence, to the left of me was a small gate, and that by passing through that gate would throw me into an open field, and give me clear running to the wood; but on looking through the gate, I saw that my captor, being with the team, would see me if I attempted to start before he moved from the position he then occupied. To add to my difficulty the horses had baulked; while waiting for the decisive moment, the boy came to the door and asked me why I did not come in. I told him I felt unwell, and wished him to be so kind as to hand me a glass of water; expecting while he was gone to get it, the team would clear, so that I could start. While he was gone, another attempt was made to start the team but failed; he came with the water and I quickly used it up by gargling my throat and by drinking a part. I asked him to serve me by giving me another glass: he gave me a look of close scrutiny, but went in for the water. I heard him fill the glass, and start to return with it; when the hind end of the waggon cleared the corner of the house, which stood in a range with the fence along which I was to pass in getting to the wood. As I passed out the gate, I "squared my main yard," and laid my course up the line of fence, I cast a last glance over my right shoulder, and saw the boy just perch his head above the garden picket to look after me; I heard at the same time great confusion with the team, the rain having made the ground slippery, and the horses having to cross the road with a slant and rise to get into the barn, it required great effort after they started to prevent their baulking. I felt some assurance that although the boy might give the alarm, my captor could not leave the team until it was in the barn. I heard the horses' feet on the barn-floor, just as I leaped the fence, and darted into the wood.

The sun was now quite down behind the western horizon, and just at this time a heavy dark curtain of clouds was let down, which seemed to usher in haste the night shade. I have never before or since seen anything which seemed to me to compare in sublimity with the spreading of the night shades at the close of that day. My reflections upon the events of that day, and upon the close of it, since I became acquainted with the Bible, have frequently brought to my mind that beautiful passage in the Book of Job, "He holdeth back the face of His throne, and spreadeth a cloud before it."

Before I proceed to the critical events and final deliverance of the next chapter, I cannot forbear to pause a moment here for reflection. The reader may well imagine how the events of the past day affected my mind. You have seen what was done to me; you have heard what was said to me--you have also seen what I have done, and heard what I have said. If you ask me whether I had expected before I left home, to gain my liberty by shedding men's blood, or breaking their limbs? I answer, no! and as evidence of this, I had provided no weapon whatever; not so much as a penknife-- it never once entered my mind. I cannot say that I expected to have the ill fortune of meeting with any human being who would attempt to impede my flight.

If you ask me if I expected when I left home to gain my liberty by fabrications and untruths? I answer, no! my parents, slaves as they were, had always taught me, when they could, that "truth may be blamed but cannot be shamed;" so far as their example was concerned, I had no habits of untruth. I was arrested, and the demand made upon me, "Who do you belong to?" knowing the fatal use these men would make of *my* truth, I at once concluded that they had no more right to it than a highwayman has to a traveller's purse.

If you ask me whether I now really believe that I gained my liberty by those lies? I answer, no! I now believe that I should be free, had I told the truth; but, at that moment, I could not see any other way to baffle my enemies, and escape their clutches.

The history of that day has never ceased to inspire me with a deeper hatred of slavery; I never recur to it but with the most intense horror at a system which can put a man not only in peril of liberty, limb, and life itself, but which may even send him in haste to the bar of God with a lie upon his lips.

Whatever my readers may think, therefore, of the history of events of the day, do not admire in it the fabrications; but *see* in it the impediments that often fall into the pathway of the flying bondman. *See* how human bloodhounds gratuitously chase, catch, and tempt him to shed blood and lie; how, when he would do good, evil is thrust upon him.

CHAPTER III.

A DREARY NIGHT IN THE WOODS--CRITICAL SITUATION THE NEXT DAY.

ALMOST immediately on entering the wood, I not only found myself embosomed in the darkness of the night, but I also found myself entangled in a thick forest of undergrowth, which had been quite thoroughly wetted by the afternoon rain.

I penetrated through the wood, thick and thin, and more or less wet, to the distance I should think of three miles. By this time my clothes were all thoroughly soaked through, and I felt once more a gloom and wretchedness; the recollection of which makes me shudder at this distant day. My young friends in this highly favoured Christian country, surrounded with all the comforts of home and parental care, visited by pastors and Sabbath-school teachers, think of the dreary condition of the blacksmith boy in the dark wood that night; and then consider that thousands of his brethren have had to undergo much greater hardships in their flight from slavery.

I was now out of the hands of those who had so cruelly teased me during the day; but a number of fearful thoughts rushed into my mind to alarm me. It was dark and cloudy, so that I could not see the *north star.* How do I know what ravenous beasts are in this wood? How do I know what precipices may be within its bounds? I cannot rest in this wood to-morrow, for it will be searched by those men from whom I have escaped; but how shall I regain the road? How shall I know when I am on the right road again?

These are some of the thoughts that filled my mind with gloom and alarm.

The Fugitive Blacksmith

At a venture I struck an angle northward in search of the road. After several hours of zigzag and laborious travel, dragging through briars, thorns and running vines, I emerged from the wood and found myself wading marshy ground and over ditches.

I can form no correct idea of the distance I travelled, but I came to a road, I should think about three o'clock in the morning. It so happened that I came out near where there was a fork in the road of three prongs.

Now arose a serious query--which is the right prong for me? I was reminded by the circumstance of a superstitious proverb among the slaves, that "the left-hand turning was unlucky," but as I had never been in the habit of placing faith in this or any similar superstition, I am not aware that it had the least weight upon my mind, as I had the same difficulty with reference to the right-hand turning. After a few moments parley with myself, I took the central prong of the road and pushed on with all my speed.

It had not cleared off, but a fresh wind had sprung up; it was chilly and searching. This with my wet clothing made me very uncomfortable; my nerves began to quiver before the searching wind. The barking of mastiffs, the crowing of fowls, and the distant rattling of market waggons, warned me that the day was approaching.

My British reader must remember that in the region where I was, we know nothing of the long hours of twilight you enjoy here. With us the day is measured more by the immediate presence of the sun, and the night by the prevalence of actual darkness.

The day dawned upon me when I was near a small house and barn, situate close to the road side. The barn was too near the road, and too small to afford secure shelter for the day; but as I cast my eye around by the dim light, I could see no wood, and no larger barn. It seemed to be an open country to a wide extent. The sun was travelling so rapidly from his eastern chamber, that ten or fifteen minutes would spread broad daylight over my track. Whether *my* deed was evil, *you* may judge, but I freely confess that I did *then* prefer darkness rather than light; I therefore took to the mow of the little barn at a great risk, as the events of the day will show. It so happened that the barn was filled with corn fodder, newly cured and lately gotten in. You are aware that however quietly one may crawl into such a bed, he is compelled to make much more noise than if it were a feather-bed; and also considerably more than if it were hay or straw. Besides inflicting upon my own excited imagination the belief that I made noise enough to be heard by the inmates of the house who were likely to be rising at the time, I had the misfortune to attract the notice of a little house-dog, such as we call in that part of the world a "fice," on account of its being not only the smallest species of the canine race, but also, because it is the most saucy, noisy, and teasing of all dogs. This little creature commenced a fierce barking. I had at once great fears that the mischievous little thing would betray me; I fully apprehended that as soon as the man of the house arose, he would come and make search in the barn. It now being entirely daylight, it was too late to retreat from this shelter, even if I could have found another; I, therefore, bedded myself down into the fodder as best I could, and entered upon the annoyances of the day, with the frail hope to sustain my mind.

It was Thursday morning; the clouds that had veiled the sky during the latter part of the previous day and the previous night were gone. It was not until about an hour after the sun rose that I heard any out-door movements about the house. As soon as I heard those movements, I was satisfied there was but one man about the house, and that he was preparing to go some distance to work for the day. This was fortunate for me; the busy movements about the yard, and especially the active preparations in the house for breakfast, silenced my unwelcome little annoyer, the fice, until after the man had gone, when he commenced afresh, and continued with occasional intermissions through the day. He made regular sallies from the house to the barn, and after smelling about, would fly back to the house, barking furiously; thus he strove most skilfully throughout the entire day to raise an alarm. There seemed to be no one about the house but one or two small children and the mother, after the man was gone. About ten o'clock my attention was gravely directed to another trial: how I could pass the day without food. The reader will remember it is Thursday, and the only regular meal I have taken since Sunday, was yesterday, in the midst of great agitation, about four o'clock; that since that I have performed my arduous night's travel. At one moment, I had nearly concluded to go and present myself at the door, and ask the woman of the house to have compassion and give me food; but then I feared the consequences might be fatal, and I resolved to suffer the day out. The wind sprang up fresh and cool; the barn being small and the crevices large, my wet clothes were dried by it, and chilled me through and through.

I cannot now, with pen or tongue, give a correct idea of the feeling of wretchedness I experienced; every nerve in my system quivered, so that not a particle of my flesh was at rest. In this way I passed the day till about the middle of the afternoon, when there seemed to be an unusual stir about the public road, which passed close by the barn. Men seemed to be passing in parties on horseback, and talking anxiously. From a word which I now and then overheard, I had not a shadow of doubt that they were in search of me. One I heard say, "I ought to catch such a fellow, the only liberty he should have for one fortnight, would be ten feet of rope." Another I heard say, "I reckon he is in that wood now." Another said, "Who would have thought that rascal was so'cute?" All this while the little fice was mingling his voice with those of the horsemen, and the noise of the horses' feet. I listened and trembled.

Just before the setting of the sun, the labouring man of the house returned, and commenced his evening duties about the house and barn; chopping wood, getting up his cow, feeding his pigs, &c., attended by the little brute, who continued barking at short intervals. He came several times into the barn below. While matters were passing thus, I heard the approach of horses again, and as they came up nearer, I was led to believe that all I had heard pass, were returning in one party. They passed the barn and halted at the house, when I recognised the voice of my old captor; addressing the labourer, he asked, "Have you seen a runaway nigger pass here to-day?"

LABOURER.--"No; I have not been at home since early this morning. Where did he come from?"

CAPTOR.--"I caught him down below here yesterday morning. I had him all day, and just at night he fooled me and got away. A party of us have been after him all day; we have been up to the line, but can't hear or see anything of him. I heard this morning where he came from. He is a blacksmith, and a stiff reward is out for him, two hundred dollars."

LAB.--"He is worth looking for."

CAP.--"I reckon so. If I get my clutches on him again, I'll mosey him down to--before I eat or sleep."

* An expression which signifies to drive in a hurry.

Reader, you may if you can, imagine what the state of my mind was at this moment. I shall make no attempt to describe it to you; to my great relief, however, the party rode off, and the labourer after finishing his work went into the house. Hope seemed now to dawn for me once more; darkness was rapidly approaching, but the moments of twilight seemed much longer than they did the evening before. At length the sable covering had spread itself over the earth. About eight o'clock, I ventured to descend from the mow of the barn into the road. The little dog the while began a furious fit of barking, so much so, that I was sure that with what his master had learned about me, he could not fail to believe I was about his premises. I quickly crossed the road, and got into an open field opposite. After stepping lightly about two hundred yards, I halted, and on listening, I heard the door open. Feeling about on the ground, I picked up two stones, and one in each hand I made off as fast as I could, but I heard nothing more that indicated pursuit, and after going some distance I discharged my encumbrance, as from the reduced state of my bodily strength, I could not afford to carry ballast.

This incident had the effect to start me under great disadvantage to make a good night's journey, as it threw me at once off the road, and compelled me to encounter at once the tedious and laborious task of beating my way across marshy fields, and to drag through woods and thickets where there were no paths.

After several hours I found my way back to the road, but the hope of making anything like clever speed was out of the question. All I could do was to keep my legs in motion, and this I continued to do with the utmost difficulty. The latter part of the night I suffered extremely from cold. There came a heavy frost; I expected at every moment to fall on the road and perish. I came to a cornfield covered with heavy shocks of Indian corn that had been cut; I went into this and got an ear, and then crept into one of the shocks; eat as much of it as I could, and thought I would rest a little and start again, but weary nature could not sustain the operation of grinding hard corn for its own nourishment, and I sunk to sleep.

When I awoke, the sun was shining around; I started with alarm, but it was too late to think of seeking any other shelter; I therefore nestled myself down, and concealed myself as best I could from the light of day. After recovering a little from my fright, I commenced again eating my whole corn. Grain by grain I worked away at it; when my jaws grew tired, as they often did, I would rest, and then begin afresh. Thus, although I began an early breakfast, I was nearly the whole of the forenoon before I had done.

Nothing of importance occurred during the day, until about the middle of the afternoon, when I was thrown into a panic by the appearance of a party of gunners, who passed near me with their dogs. After shooting one or two birds, however, and passing within a few rods of my frail covering, they went on, and left me once more in hope. Friday night came without any other incident worth naming. As I sallied out, I felt evident benefit from the ear of corn I had nibbled away. My strength was considerably renewed; though I was far from being nourished, I felt that my life was at least safe from death by hunger. Thus encouraged, I set out with better speed than I had made since Sunday and Monday night. I had a presentiment, too, that I must be near free soil. I had not yet the least idea where I should find a home or a friend, still my spirits were so highly elated, that I took the whole of the road to myself; I ran, hopped, skipped, jumped, clapped my hands, and talked to myself. But to the old slaveholder I had left, I said, "Ah! ha! old fellow, I told you I'd fix you."

After an hour or two of such freaks of joy, a gloom would come over me in connexion with these questions, "But where are you going? What are you going to do? What will you do with freedom without father, mother, sisters, and brothers? What will you say when you are asked where you were born? You know nothing of the world; how will you explain the fact of your ignorance?"

These questions made me feel deeply the magnitude of the difficulties yet before me.

Saturday morning dawned upon me; and although my strength seemed yet considerably fresh, I began to feel a hunger somewhat more destructive and pinching, if possible, than I had before. I resolved, at all risk, to continue my travel by day-light, and to ask information of the first person I met.

The events of the next chapter will shew what fortune followed this resolve.

CHAPTER IV.

THE GOOD WOMAN OF THE TOLL-GATE DIRECTS ME TO W. W.--MY RECEPTION BY HIM.

THE resolution of which I informed the reader at the close of the last chapter, being put into practice, I continued my flight on the public road; and a little after the sun rose, I came in sight of a toll-gate again. For a moment all the events which followed my passing a toll-gate on Wednesday morning, came fresh to my recollection, and produced some hesitation; but at all events, said I, I will try again.

On arriving at the gate, I found it attended by an elderly woman, whom I afterwards learned was a widow, and an excellent Christian woman. I asked her if I was in Pennsylvania. On being informed that I was, I asked her if she knew where I could get employ? She said she did not; but advised me to go to W. W., a Quaker, who lived about three miles from her, whom I would find to take an interest in me. She gave me directions which way to take; I thanked her, and bade her good morning, and was very careful to follow her directions.

In about half an hour I stood trembling at the door of W. W. After knocking, the door opened upon a comfortably spread table; the sight of which seemed at once to increase my hunger sevenfold. Not daring to enter, I said I had been sent to him in search of employ. "Well," said he, "Come in and take thy breakfast, and get warm, and we will talk about it; thee must be cold without any coat." *"Come in and take thy breakfast, and get warm!,"* These words spoken by a stranger, but with such an air of simple sincerity and fatherly kindness, made an overwhelming impression upon my mind. They made me feel, spite of all my fear and timidity that I had in the providence of God, found a friend and a home. He at once gained my confidence; and I felt that I might confide to him a fact which I had, as yet, confided to no one.

From that day to this, whenever I discover the least disposition in my heart to disregard the wretched condition of any poor or distressed persons with whom I meet, I call to mind these words--*"Come in and take thy breakfast, and get warm."* They invariably remind me of what I was at that time; my condition was as wretched as that of any human being can possibly be, with the exception of the loss of health or reason. I had but four pieces of clothing about my person, having left all the rest in the hands of my captors. I was a starving fugitive, without home or friends--a reward offered for my person in the public papers--pursued by cruel manhunters, and no claim upon him to whose door I went. Had he turned me away, I must have perished. Nay, he took me in, and gave me of his food, and shared with me his own garments. Such treatment I had never before received at the hands of any white man.

A few such men in slaveholding America, have stood, and even now stand, like Abrahams and Lots, to stay its forthcoming and well-earned and just judgment.

The limits of this work compel me to pass over many interesting incidents which occurred during my six months' concealment in that family. I must confine myself only to those which will show the striking providence of God, in directing my steps to the door of W. W., and how great an influence the incidents of that six months has had upon all my subsequent history. My friend kindly gave me employ to saw and split a number of cords of wood, then lying in his yard, for which he agreed with me for liberal pay and board. This inspired me with great encouragement. The idea of beginning to earn something was very pleasant. Next; we confidentially agreed upon the way and means of avoiding surprise, in case any one should come to the house as a spy, or with intention to arrest me. This afforded still further relief, as it convinced me that the whole family would now be on the look out for such persons.

The next theme of conversation was with reference to my education.

"Can thee read or write any, James?" was the question put to me the morning after my arrival, by W. W.

"No, sir, I cannot; my duties as a blacksmith have made me acquainted with the figures on the common mechanics' square. There was a day-book kept in the shop, in which the overseer usually charged the smithwork we did for the neighbours. I have spent entire Sabbaths looking over the pages of that book; knowing the names of persons to whom certain pieces of work were charged, together with their prices, I strove anxiously to learn to write in this way. I got paper, and picked up feathers about the yard, and made ink of--berries. My quills being too soft, and my skill in making a pen so poor, that

I undertook some years ago to make a steel pen.

* This attempt was as early as 1822.

In this way I have learnt to make a few of the letters, but I cannot write my own name, nor do I know the letters of the alphabet."

W. W., (handing a slate and pencil.)--"Let me see how thee makes letters; try such as thou hast been able to make easily."

A. B. C. L. G.

P. W., (wife of W. W.)--"Why, those are better than I can make."

W. W.--"Oh, we can soon get thee in the way, James."

Arithmetic and astronomy became my favourite studies. W. W. was an accomplished scholar; he had been a teacher for some years, and was cultivating a small farm on account of ill-health, which had compelled him to leave teaching. He is one of the most far-sighted and practical men I ever met with. He taught me by familiar conversations, illustrating his themes by diagrams on the slate, so that I caught his ideas with ease and rapidity.

I now began to see, for the first time, the extent of the mischief slavery had done to me. Twenty-one years of my life were gone, never again to return, and I was as profoundly ignorant, comparatively, as a child five years old. This was painful, annoying, and humiliating in the extreme. Up to this time, I recollected to have seen one copy of the New Testament, but the entire Bible I had never seen, and had never heard of the Patriarchs, or of the Lord Jesus Christ. I recollected to have heard two sermons, but had heard no mention in them of Christ, or the way of life by Him. It is quite easy to imagine, then, what was the state of my mind, having been reared in total moral midnight; it was a sad picture of mental and spiritual darkness.

As my friend poured light into my mind, I saw the darkness; it amazed and grieved me beyond description.

Sometimes I sank down under the load, and became discouraged, and dared not hope that I could ever succeed in acquiring knowledge enough to make me happy, or useful to my fellow-beings.

My dear friend, W. W., however, had a happy tact to inspire me with confidence; and he, perceiving my state of mind, exerted himself, not without success, to encourage me. He cited to me various instances of coloured persons, of whom I had not heard before, and who had distinguished themselves for learning, such as Bannicker, Wheatley, and Francis Williams.

How often have I regretted that the six months I spent in the family of W. W., could not have been six years. The danger of recapture, however, rendered it utterly imprudent that I should remain longer; and early in the month of March, while the ground was covered with the winter's snow, I left the bosom of this excellent family, and went forth once more to try my fortune among strangers.

My dear reader, if I could describe to you the emotions I felt when I left the threshold of W. W.'s door, you could not fail to see how deplorable is the condition of the fugitive slave, often for months and years after he has escaped the immediate grasp of the tyrant. When I left my parents, the trial was great, but I had now to leave a friend who had done more for me than parents could have done as slaves; and hence I felt an endearment to that friend which was heightened by a sense of the important relief he had afforded me in the greatest need, and hours of pleasant and highly profitable intercourse.

About a month previous to leaving the house of W. W., a small circumstance occurred one evening, which I only name to shew the harassing fears and dread in which I lived during most of the time I was there. He had a brother-in-law living some ten miles distant--he was a friend to the slave; he often came unexpectedly and spent a few hours--sometimes a day and a night. I had not, however, ever known him to come at night. One night about nine o'clock, after I had gone to bed, (my lodging being just over the room in which W. W. and his wife were sitting,) I heard the door open and a voice ask, "Where is the boy?" The voice sounded to me like the voice of my master; I was sure it must be his. I sprang and listened for a moment--it seemed to be silent; I heard nothing, and then it seemed to me there was a confusion. There was a window at the head of my bed, which I could reach without getting upon the floor: it was a single sash and opened upon hinges. I quickly opened this window and waited in a perfect tremour of dread for further development. There was a door at the foot of the stairs; as I heard that door open, I sprang for the window, and my head was just out, when the gentle voice of my friend W. W. said, "James?"

* If W. W. had ascended the stairs without calling, I should certainly have jumped out of the window.

"Here," said I, "----has come, and he would like to have thee put up his horse." I drew a breath of relief, but my strength and presence of mind did not return for some hours. I slept none that night; for a moment I could doze away, but the voice would sound in my ears, "Where is that boy?" and it would seem to me it must be the tyrant in quest of his weary prey, and would find myself starting again.

From that time the agitation of my mind became so great that I could not feel myself safe. Every day seemed to increase my fear, till I was unfit for work, study or rest. My friend endeavoured, but in vain, to get me to stay a week longer.

The events of the spring proved that I had not left too soon. As soon as the season for travelling fairly opened, active search was made, and my master was seen in a town, twenty miles in advance of where I had spent my six months.

The following curious fact also came out. That same brother-in-law who frightened me, was putting up one evening at a hotel some miles off, and while sitting quietly by himself in one part of the room, he overheard a conversation between a travelling pedler and several gossippers of the neighbourhood, who were lounging away the evening at the hotel.

PEDLER.--"Do you know one W. W. somewhere about here?"

GOSSIPER.--"Yes, he lives ---- miles off."

PED.--"I understand he had a black boy with him last winter, I wonder if he is there yet?"

GOS.--"I don't know, he most always has a runaway nigger with him."

PED.--"I should like to find out whether that fellow is there yet."

BROTHER-IN-LAW, (turning about.)--"What does thee know about that boy?"

PED.--"Well he is a runaway."

BROTHER-IN-LAW.--"Who did he run away from?"

PED.--"From Col---- in ----."

BROTHER-IN-LAW.--"How did thee find out that fact?"

PED.--"Well, I have been over there peddling."

BROTHER-IN-LAW.--"Where art thou from?"

PED.--"I belong in Conn."

BROTHER-IN-LAW.--"Did thee see the boy's master?"

PED.--"Yes."

BROTHER-IN-LAW.--"What did he offer thee to find the boy?"

PED.--"I agreed to find out where he was, and let him know, and if he got him, I was to receive----."

BROTHER-IN-LAW.--"How didst thou hear the boy had been with W. W."

PED.--"Oh, he is known to be a notorious rascal for enticing away, and concealing slaves; he'll get himself into trouble yet, the slaveholders are on the look out for him."

BROTHER-IN-LAW.--"W. W. is my brother-in-law; the boy of whom thou speakest is not with him, and to save thee the trouble of abusing him, I can moreover say, he is no rascal."

PED.--"He may not be there now, but it is because he has sent him off. His master heard of him, and from the description, he is sure it must have been his boy. He could tell me pretty nigh where he was; he said he was a fine healthy boy, twenty-one, a first-rate blacksmith; he would not have taken a thousand dollars for him."

BROTHER-IN-LAW.--"I know not where the boy is, but I have no doubt he is worth more to himself than he ever was to his master, high as he fixes the price on him; and I have no doubt thee will do better to pursue thy peddling honestly, than to neglect it for the sake of serving negro-hunters at a venture."

All this happened within a month or two after I left my friend. One fact which makes this part of the story deeply interesting to my own mind, is, that some years elapsed before it came to my knowledge.

CHAPTER V.

SEVEN MONTHS' RESIDENCE IN THE FAMILY OF J. K. A MEMBER OF THE SOCIETY OF FRIENDS, IN CHESTER COUNTY, PENNSYLVANIA.--REMOVAL TO NEW YORK--BECOMES A CONVERT TO RELIGION--BECOMES A TEACHER.

ON leaving W. W., I wended my way in deep sorrow and melancholy, onward towards Philadelphia, and after travelling two days and a night, I found shelter and employ in the family of J. K., another member of the Society of Friends, a farmer.

The religious atmosphere in this family was excellent. Mrs. K. gave me the first copy of the Holy Scriptures I ever possessed, she also gave me much excellent counsel. She was a preacher in the Society of Friends; this occasioned her with her husband to be much of their time from home. This left the charge of the farm upon me, and besides put it out of their power to render me that aid in my studies which my former friend had. I, however, kept myself closely concealed, by confining myself to the limits of the farm, and using all my leisure time in study. This place was more secluded, and I felt less of dread and fear of discovery than I had before, and although seriously embarrassed for want of an instructor, I realized some pleasure and profit in my studies. I often employed myself in drawing rude maps of the solar system, and diagrams illustrating the theory of solar eclipses. I felt also a fondness for reading the

[1850 edition used to supply missing pages 50 and 51 of 1849 edition.]

Bible, and committing chapters, and verse of hymns to memory. Often on the Sabbath when alone in the barn, I would break the monotony of the hours by endeavouring to speak, as if I was addressing an audience. My mind was constantly struggling for thought, and I was still more grieved and alarmed at its barrenness; I found it gradually freed from the darkness entailed by slavery, but I was deeply and anxiously concerned how I should fill it with useful knowledge. I had a few books, and no tutor.

In this way I spent seven months with J. K., and should have continued longer, agreeably to his urgent solicitation, but I felt that life was fast wearing, and that as I was now free, I must adventure in search of knowledge. On leaving J. K., he kindly gave me the following certificate,--

East Nautmeal, Chester County, Pennsylvania,
Tenth Month 5th, 1828

"I hereby certify, that the bearer, J. W. C. Pennington, has been in my employ seven months, during most of which time I have been from home, leaving my entire business in his trust, and that he has proved a highly trustworthy and industrious young man. He leaves with the sincere regret of myself and family; but as he feels it to be his duty to go where he can obtain education, so as to fit him to be more useful, I cordially commend him to the warm sympathy of the friends of humanity wherever a wise providence may appoint him a home.

Signed, "J. K."

Passing through Philadelphia, I went to New York, and in a short time found employ on Long Island, near the city. At this time, the state of things was extremely critical in New York. It was just two years after the general emancipation in that state. In the city it was a daily occurrence for slaveholders from the southern states to catch their slaves, and by certificate from Recorder Riker take them back. I often felt serious apprehensions of danger, and yet I felt also that I must begin the world somewhere.

I was earning respectable wages, and by means of evening schools and private tuition, was making encouraging progress in my studies.

Up to this time, it had never occurred to me that I was a slave in another and a more serious sense. All my serious impression of mind had been with reference to the slavery from which I had escaped. Slavery had been my theme of thought day and night.

In the spring of 1829, I found my mind unusually perplexed about the state of the slave. I was enjoying rare privileges in attending a Sabbath school; the great value of Christian knowledge began to be impressed upon my mind to an extent I had not been conscious of before. I began to contrast my condition with that of ten brothers and sisters I had left in slavery, and the condition of children I saw sitting around me on the Sabbath, with their pious teachers, with that of 700,000, now 800,440 slave children, who had no means of Christian instruction.

The theme was more powerful than any my mind had ever encountered before. It entered into the deep chambers of my soul, and stirred the most agitating emotions I had ever felt. The question was, what can I do for that vast body of suffering brotherhood I have left behind. To add to the weight and magnitude of the theme, I learnt for the first time how many slaves there were. The question completely staggered my mind; and finding myself more and more borne down with it, until I was in an agony; I thought I would make it a subject of prayer to God, although prayer had not been my habit, having never attempted it but once.

I not only prayed, but also fasted. It was while engaged thus, that my attention was seriously drawn to the fact that I was a lost sinner, and a slave to Satan; and soon I saw that I must make another escape from another tyrant. I did not by any means forget my fellow-bondmen, of whom I had been sorrowing so deeply, and travailing in spirit so earnestly; but I now saw that while man had been injuring me, I had been offending God; and that unless I ceased to offend him, I could not expect to have his sympathy in my wrongs; and moreover, that I could not be instrumental in eliciting his powerful aid in behalf of those for whom I mourned so deeply.

This may provoke a smile from some who profess to be the friends of the slave, but who have a lower estimate of experimental Christianity than I believe is due to it; but I am not the less confident that sincere prayer to God, proceeding from a few hearts deeply imbued with experimental Christianity about *that time,* has had much to do with subsequent happy results. At that time the 800,000 bondmen in the British Isles had not seen the beginning of the end of their sufferings--at that time, 20,000 who are now free in Canada, were in bonds--at that time, there was no Vigilance Committee to aid the flying slave--at that time, the two powerful Anti-Slavery Societies of America had no being.

I distinctly remember that I felt the need of enlisting the sympathy of God, in behalf of my enslaved brethren; but when I attempted it day after day, and night after night, I was made to feel, that whatever else I might do, I was not qualified to do that, as I was myself alienated from him by wicked works. In short, I felt that I needed the powerful aid of some in my behalf with God, just as much as I did that of my dear friend in Pennsylvania, when flying from man. "If one man sin against another, the judge shall judge him, but if a man sin against God, who shall entreat for him?"

Day after day, for about two weeks, I found myself more deeply convicted of personal guilt before God. My heart, soul and body were in the greatest distress; I thought of neither food, drink or rest, for days and nights together. Burning with a recollection of the wrongs man had done me--mourning for the injuries my brethren were still enduring, and deeply convicted of the guilt of my own sins against God. One evening, in the third week of the struggle, while alone in my chamber, and after solemn reflection for several hours, I concluded that I could never be happy or useful in that state of mind, and resolved that I would try to become reconciled to God. I was then living in the family of an Elder of the Presbyterian Church. I had not made known my feelings to any one, either in the family or out of it; and I did not suppose that any one had discovered my feelings. To my surprise, however, I found that the family had not only been aware of my state for several days, but were deeply anxious on my behalf. The following Sabbath, Dr. Cox was on a visit in Brooklyn to preach, and was a guest in the family; hearing of my case, he expressed a wish to converse with me, and without out knowing the plan, I was invited into a room and left alone with him. He entered skilfully and kindly into my feelings, and after considerable conversation he invited me to attend his service that afternoon. I did so, and was deeply interested.

Without detaining the reader with too many particulars, I will only state that I heard the doctor once or twice after this, at his own place of worship in New York City, and had several personal interviews with him, as the result of which, I hope, I was brought to a saving acquaintance with Him, of whom Moses in the Law and the Prophets did write; and soon connected myself with the church under his pastoral care.

I now returned with all my renewed powers to the great theme--slavery. It seemed now as I looked at it, to be more hideous than ever. I saw it now as an evil under the moral government of God--as a sin not only against man, but also against God. The great and engrossing thought with me was, how shall I now employ my time and my talents so as to tell most effectually upon this system of wrong! As I have stated, there was no Anti-Slavery Society then--there was no Vigilance Committee. I had, therefore, to select a course of action, without counsel or advice from any one who professed to sympathize with the slave. Many, many lonely hours of deep meditation have I passed during the years 1828 and 1829, before the great anti-slavery movement. On the questions, What shall I do for the slave? How shall I act so that he will reap the benefit of my time and talents? At one time I had resolved to go to Africa, and to react from there; but without bias or advice from any mortal, I soon gave up that, as looking too much like feeding a hungry man with a long spoon.

At length, finding that the misery, ignorance, and wretchedness of the free coloured people was by the whites tortured into an argument for slavery; finding myself now among the free people of colour in New York, where slavery was so recently abolished; and finding much to do for their elevation, I resolved to give my strength in that direction. And well do I remember the great movement which commenced among us about this time, for the holding of General Conventions, to devise ways and means for their elevation, which continued with happy influence up to 1834, when we gave way to anti-slavery friends, who had then taken up the labouring oar. And well do I remember that the first time I ever saw those tried friends, Garrison, Jocelyn, and Tappan, was in one of those Conventions, where they came to make our acquaintance, and to secure our confidence in some of their preliminary labours.

My particular mode of labour was still a subject of deep reflection; and from time to time I carried it to the Throne of Grace. Eventually my mind fixed upon the ministry as the desire of my whole heart. I had mastered the preliminary branches of English education, and was engaged in studying logic, rhetoric, and the Greek Testament, without a master. While thus struggling in my laudable work, an opening presented itself which was not less surprising than gratifying. Walking on the street one day, I met a friend, who said to me, "I have just had an application to supply a teacher for a school, and I have recommended you." I said, "My dear friend, I am obliged to you for the kindness; but I fear I cannot sustain an examination for that station." "Oh," said he, "try." I said, "I will," and we separated. Two weeks afterwards, I met the trustees of the school, was examined, accepted, and agreed with them for a salary of two hundred dollars per annum; commenced my school, and succeeded. This was five years, three months, and thirteen days after I came from the South.

As the events of my life since that have been of a public professional nature, I will say no more about it. My object in writing this tract is now completed. It has been to shew the reader the hand of God with a slave; and to elicit your sympathy in behalf of the fugitive slave, by shewing some of the untold dangers and hardships through which he has to pass to gain liberty, and how much he needs friends on free soil; and that men who have felt the yoke of slavery, even in its mildest form, cannot be expected to speak of the system otherwise than in terms of the most unqualified condemnation.

There is one sin that slavery committed against me, which I never can forgive. It robbed me of my education; the injury is irreparable; I feel the embarrassment more seriously now than I ever did before. It cost me two years' hard labour, after I fled, to unshackle my mind; it was three years before I had purged my language of slavery's idioms; it was four years before I had thrown off the crouching aspect of slavery; and now the evil that besets me is a great lack of that general information, the foundation of which is most effectually laid in that part of life which I served as a slave. When I consider how much now, more than ever, depends upon sound and thorough education among coloured men, I am grievously overwhelmed with a sense of my deficiency, and more especially as I can never hope now to make it up. If I know my own heart, I have no ambition but to serve the cause of suffering humanity; all that I have desired or sought, has been to make me more efficient for good. So far I have some consciousness that I have done my utmost; and should my future days be few or many, I am reconciled to meet the last account, hoping to be acquitted of any wilful neglect of duty; but I shall have to go to my last account with this charge against the system of slavery, *"Vile monster! thou hast hindered my usefulness, by robbing me of my early education."*

Oh! what might I have been now, but for this robbery perpetrated upon me as soon as I saw the light. When the monster heard that a man child was born, he laughed, and said, "It is mine." When I was laid in the cradle, he came and looked on my face, and wrote down my name upon his barbarous list of chattels personal, on the same list where he registered his horses, hogs, cows, sheep, and even his *dogs!* Gracious Heaven, is there no repentance for the misguided men who do these things!

The only harm I wish to slaveholders is, that they may be speedily delivered from the guilt of a sin, which, if not repented of, must bring down the judgment of Almighty God upon their devoted heads. The least I desire for the slave is, that he may be speedily released from the pain of drinking a cup whose bitterness I have sufficiently tasted, to know that it is insufferable.

CHAPTER VI.

SOME ACCOUNT OF THE FAMILY I LEFT IN SLAVERY--PROPOSAL TO PURCHASE MYSELF AND PARENTS--HOW MET BY MY OLD MASTER.

IT is but natural that the reader should wish to hear a word about the family I left behind.

There are frequently large slave families with whom God seems to deal in a remarkable manner. I believe my family is an instance.

I have already stated that when I fled, I left a father, mother, and eleven brothers and sisters. These were all, except my oldest brother, owned by the man from whom I fled. It will be seen at once then how the fear of implicating them embarrassed me in the outset. They suffered nothing, however, but a strong suspicion, until about six months after I had left; when the following circumstance took place:--

When I left my friend W. W. in Pennsylvania to go on north, I ventured to write a letter back to one of my brothers, informing him how I was; and this letter was directed to the care of a white man who was hired on the plantation, who worked in the garden with my father, and who professed a warm friendship to our family; but instead of acting in good faith, he handed the letter to my master. I am sorry that truth compels me to say that that man was an Englishman.

From that day the family were handled most strangely. The history begins thus: they were all sold into Virginia, the adjoining state. This was done lest I should have some plan to get them off; but God so ordered that they fell into kinder hands. After a few years, however, their master became much

embarrassed, so that he was obliged to pass them into other hands, at least for a term of years. By this change the family was divided, and my parents, with the greater part of their children, were taken to New Orleans. After remaining there several years at hard labour,--my father being in a situation of considerable trust, they were again taken back to Virginia; and by this means became entitled by the laws of that state to their freedom. Before justice, however, could take its course, their old master in Maryland, as if intent to doom them for ever to bondage, repurchased them; and in order to defeat a similar law in Maryland, by which they would have been entitled to liberty, he obtained from the General Assembly of that state the following special act. This will show not only something of his character as a slaveholder, but also his political influence in the state. It is often urged in the behalf of slaveholders, that the law interposes an obstacle in the way of emancipating their slaves when they wish to do so, but here is an instance which lays open the real philosophy of the whole case. They make the law themselves, and when they find the laws operate more in favour of the slaves than themselves, they can easily evade or change it. Maryland being a slave-exporting state, you will see why they need a law to prohibit the importation of slaves; it is a protection to that sort of trade. This law he wished to evade.

"An act for the Relief of ---- of ---- County. Passed January **17th, 1842.**

"Whereas it is represented to this General Assembly that ---- of ---- county, brought into this state from the state of Virginia, sometime in the month of March last, two negro slaves, to wit,----

and ---- his wife, who are slaves for life, and who were acquired by the said ---- by purchase, and whereas, the said ---- is desirous of retaining said slaves in this state. THEREFORE, BE IT ENACTED, *by the General Assembly* of Maryland, that the said ---- be, and he is hereby authorized to retain said negroes as slaves for life within this state, provided that the said ---- shall within thirty days after the passage of this act, file with the clerk of the ---- county court, a list of said slaves so brought into this state, stating their ages, with an affidavit thereto attached, that the same is a true and faithful list of the slaves so removed, and that they were not brought into this state for the purpose of sale, and that they are slaves for life. And *provided also,* that the sum of fifteen dollars for each slave, between the ages of twelve and forty-five years, and the sum of five dollars for each slave above the age of forty-five years and under twelve years of age, so brought into this state, shall be paid to the said clerk of ---- county court: to be paid over by him to the treasurer of the western shore, for the use and benefit of the Colonization Society of this state.

State of Connecticut.
Office of Secretary of State.

"I hereby certify, that the foregoing is a true copy of an act passed by the General Assembly of Maryland, January 17th, 1842, as it appears in the printed acts of the said Maryland, in the Library of the state.

In testimony whereof, I have hereunto set my hand and seal of said state, at Hartford, this 17th day of August, 1846.

(SEAL.)

CHARLES W. BEADLEY,
Secretary of State.

Thus, the whole family after being twice fairly entitled to their liberty, even by the laws of two slave states, had the mortification of finding themselves again, not only recorded as slaves for life, but also a premium paid upon them, professedly to aid in establishing others of their fellow-beings in a free republic on the coast of Africa; but the hand of God seems to have been heavy upon the man who could plan such a stratagem to wrong his fellows.

The immense fortune he possessed when I left him, (bating one thousand dollars I brought with me in my own body,) and which he seems to have retained till that time, began to fly, and in a few years he was insolvent, so that he was unable to hold the family, and was compelled to think of selling them again. About this time I heard of their state by an underground railroad passenger, who came from that neighbourhood, and resolved to make an effort to obtain the freedom of my parents, and to relieve myself from liability. For this purpose, after arranging for the means to purchase, I employed counsel to make a definite offer for my parents and myself. To his proposal, the following evasive and offensive answer was returned.

January 12*th*, 1846.

J. H.--, Esq.

"Sir,--Your letter is before me. The ungrateful servant in whose behalf you write, merits no clemency from me. He was guilty of theft when he departed, for which I hope he has made due amends. I have heard he was a respectable man, and calculated to do some good to his fellow-beings. Servants are selling from five hundred and fifty to seven hundred dollars. I will take five hundred and fifty dollars, and liberate

him. If my proposition is acceded to, and the money lodged in Baltimore, I will execute the necessary instrument, and deliver it in Baltimore, to be given up on payment being made.

"Yours, &c.,

"----."

Here he not only refuses to account for my parents, by including them in his return and proposition, but he at the same time attempts to intimidate me by mooting the charge of theft.

I confess I was not only surprised, but mortified, at this result. The hope of being once more united to parents whom I had not seen for sixteen years, and whom I still loved dearly, had so excited my mind, that I disarranged my business relations, disposed of a valuable library of four hundred volumes, and by additional aid obtained among the liberal people of Jamaica, I was prepared to give the extravagant sum of five hundred dollars each for myself, and my father and mother. This I was willing to do, not because I approve of the principle involved as a general rule. But supposing that, as my former master was now an old man not far from his grave, (about which I was not mistaken) and as he knew, by his own shewing, that I was able to do some good, he would be inclined, whatever might have been our former relations and misunderstandings, to meet my reasonable desire to see my parents, and to part this world in reconciliation with each other, as well as with God. I should have rejoiced had his temper permitted him to accede to my offer. But I thought it too bad, a free man of Jesus Christ, living on "free soil," to give a man five hundred dollars for the privilege of being let alone, and to be branded as a thief into the bargain, and that too after I had served him twenty prime years, without the benefit of being taught so much as the alphabet.

I wrote him with my own hand, sometime after this, stating that no proposition would be acceded to by me, which did not include my parents; and likewise fix the sum for myself more reasonable, and also retract the offensive charge; to this he maintained a dignified silence. The means I had acquired by the contributions of kind friends to redeem myself, I laid by, in case the worst should come; and that designed for the purchase of my parents, I used in another kind of operation, as the result of which, my father and two brothers are now in Canada. My mother was sold a second time, south, but she was eventually found. Several of my sisters married free men, who purchased their liberty; and three brothers are owned, by what may be called conscience slaveholders, who hold slaves only for a term of years. My old master has since died; my mother and he are now in the other world together, she is at rest from him. Sometime after his death, I received information from a gentleman, intimate with his heirs, (who are principally females) that the reduced state of the family, afforded not only a good opportunity to obtain a release upon reasonable terms, but also to render the children of my oppressor some pecuniary aid; and much as I had suffered, I must confess this latter was the stronger motive with me, for acceding to their offer made by him.

I have many other deeply interesting particulars

touching our family history, but I have detailed as many as prudence will permit, on account of those members who are yet south of Mason and Dixon's line.

I have faith in the hand that has dealt with us so strangely, that all our remaining members will in time be brought together; and then the case may merit a reviewed and enlarged edition of this tract, when other important matter will be inserted.

CHAPTER VII.

THE FEEDING AND CLOTHING OF THE SLAVES IN THE PART OF MARYLAND WHERE I LIVED, &c.

THE slaves are generally fed upon salt pork, herrings and Indian corn.

The manner of dealing it out to them is as follows:-- Each working man, on Monday morning, goes to the cellar of the master where the provisions are kept, and where the overseer takes his stand with some one to assist him, when he, with a pair of steel-yards, weighs out to every man the amount of three-and-a-half pounds, to last him till the ensuing Monday--allowing him just half-a-pound per day. Once in a few weeks there is a change made, by which, instead of the three-and-a-half pounds of pork, each man receives twelve herrings, allowing two a-day. The only bread kind the slaves have is that made of Indian meal. In some of the lower counties, the masters usually give their slaves the corn in the ear; and they have to grind it for themselves by night at hand-mills. But my master had a quantity sent to the grist mill at a time, to be ground into coarse meal, and kept it in a large chest in his cellar, where the woman who cooked for the boys could get it daily. This was baked in large loaves, called "steel poun bread." Sometimes as a change it was made into "Johnny Cake," and then at others into mush.

The slaves had no butter, coffee, tea, or sugar; occasionally they were allowed milk, but not statedly; the only exception to this statement was the "harvest provisions." In harvest, when cutting the grain, which lasted from two to three weeks in the heat of summer, they were allowed some fresh meat, rice, sugar, and coffee; and also their allowance of whiskey.

At the beginning of winter, each slave had one pair of coarse shoes and stockings, one pair of pantaloons, and a jacket.

At the beginning of summer, he had two pair of coarse linen pantaloons and two shirts.

Once in a number of years, each slave, or each man and his wife, had one coarse blanket and enough coarse linen for a "bed-tick." He never had any bedstead or other furniture kind. The men had no hats, waistcoats or handkerchiefs given them, or the women any bonnets. These they had to contrive for themselves. Each labouring man had a small "patch" of ground allowed him; from this he was expected to furnish himself and his boys hats, &c. These patches they had to work by night; from these, also, they had to raise their own provisions, as no potatoes, cabbage, &c., were allowed them from the plantation. Years ago the slaves were in the habit of raising broom-corn, and making brooms to supply the market in the towns; but now of later years great quantities of these and other articles, such as scrubbing-brushes, wooden trays, mats, baskets, and straw hats which the slaves made, are furnished by the shakers and other small manufacturers, from the free states of the north.

Neither my master or any other master, within my acquaintance, made any provisions for the religious instruction of his slaves. They were not worked on the Sabbath. One of the "boys" was required to stay at home and, "feed," that is, take care of the stock, every Sabbath; the rest went to see their friends. Those men whose families were on other plantations usually spent the Sabbath with them; some would lie about at home and rest themselves.

When it was pleasant weather my master would ride "into town" to church, but I never knew him to say a word to one of us about going to church, or about our obligations to God, or a future state. But there were a number of pious slaves in our neighbourhood, and several of these my master owned; one of these was an exhorter. He was not connected with a religious body, but used to speak every Sabbath in some part of the neighbourhood. When slaves died, their remains were usually consigned to the grave without any ceremony, but this old gentleman, wherever he heard of a slave having been buried in that way, would send notice from plantation to plantation, calling the slaves together at the grave on the Sabbath, where he'd sing, pray, and exhort. I have known him to go ten or fifteen miles voluntarily to attend these services. He could not read, and I never heard him refer to any Scripture, and state and discourse upon any fundamental doctrine of the gospel; but he knew a number of "spiritual songs by heart," of these he would give two lines at a time very exact, set and lead the tune himself; he would pray with great fervour and his exhortations were amongst the most impressive I have heard.

The Methodists at one time attempted to evangelize the slaves in our neighbourhod, but the effort was sternly resisted by the masters. They held a Camp Meeting in the neighbourhood, where many of the slaves attended. But one of their preachers for addressing words of comfort to the slaves, was arrested and tried for his life.

My master was very active in this disgraceful affair, but the excellent man, Rev. Mr. G., was acquitted and escaped out of their hands. Still, it was deemed by his brethren to be imprudent for him to preach any more in the place, as some of the more reckless masters swore violence against him. This good man's name is remembered dearly, till this day, by slaves in that county. I met with a fugitive about a year ago, who remembered distinctly the words spoken by Mr. G., and by which his own mind was awakened to a sense of the value of his soul. He said, in the course of his preaching, addressing himself to the slaves, "You have precious immortal souls, that are worth far more to you than your bodies are to your masters;" or words to that effect. But while these words interested many slaves, they also made many masters exceedingly angry, and they tortured his words into an attempt to excite the slaves to rebellion.

Some of my master's slaves who had families, were regularly married, and others were not; the law makes no provision for such marriages, and the only provision made by the master was, that they should obtain his leave. In some cases, after obtaining leave to take his wife, the slave would ask further leave to go to a minister and be married. I never knew him to deny such a request, and yet, in those cases where the slave did not ask it, he never required him to be married by a minister. Of course, no Bibles, Tracts, or religious books of any kind, were ever given to the slaves; and no ministers or religious instructors were ever known to visit our plantation at any time, either in sickness or in health. When a slave was sick, my master being

himself a physician, sometimes attended, and sometimes he called other physicians. Slaves frequently sickened and died, but I never knew any provision made to administer to them the comforts, or to offer to them the hopes of the gospel, or to their friends after their death.

There is no one feature of slavery to which the mind recurs with more gloomy impressions, than to its disastrous influence upon the families of the masters, physically, pecuniarily, and mentally.

It seems to destroy families as by a powerful blight, large and opulent slave-holding families, often vanish like a group of shadows at the third or fourth generation. This fact arrested my attention some years before I escaped from slavery, and of course before I had any enlightened views of the moral character of the system. As far back as I can recollect, indeed, it was a remark among slaves, that every generation of slaveholders are more and more inferior. There were several large and powerful families in our county, including that of my master, which affords to my mind a melancholy illustration of this remark. One of the wealthiest slaveholders in the county, was General R., a brother-in-law to my master. This man owned a large and highly valuable tract of land, called R.'s Manor. I do not know how many slaves he owned, but the number was large. He lived in a splendid mansion, and drove his coach and four. He was for some years a member of Congress. He had a numerous family of children.

The family showed no particular signs of decay until he had married a second time, and had considerably

increased his number of children. It then became evident that his older children were not educated for active business, and were only destined to be a charge. Of sons, (seven or eight,) not one of them reached the eminence once occupied by the father. The only one that approached to it, was the eldest, who became an officer in the navy, and obtained the doubtful glory of being killed in the Mexican war.

General R. himself ran through his vast estate, died intemperate, and left a widow and large number of daughters, some minors, destitute, and none of his sons fitted for any employment but in the army and navy.

Slaves have a superstitious dread of passing the dilapidated dwelling of a man who has been guilty of great cruelties to his slaves, and who is dead, or moved away. I never felt this dread deeply but once, and that was one Sabbath about sunset, as I crossed the yard of General R.'s residence, which was about two miles from us, after he had been compelled to leave it.

To see the once fine smooth gravel walks, overgrown with grass--the redundances of the shrubbery neglected--the once finely painted pricket fences, rusted and fallen down--a fine garden in splendid ruins--the lofty ceiling of the mansion thickly curtained with cobwebs--the spacious apartments abandoned, while the only music heard within as a substitute for the voices of family glee that once filled it, was the crying cricket and cockroaches! Ignorant slave as I was at that time, I could but pause for a moment, and recur in silent horror to the fact that, a strange reverse of fortune, had lately driven from that proud mansion, a large and once opulent family. What advantage was it now to the members of that family, that the father and head had for near half a century stood high in the counsels of the state, and had the benefit of the unrequited toil of hundreds of his fellowmen, when they were already grappling with the annoyances of that poverty, which he had entailed upon others.

My master's family, in wealth and influence, was not inferior to General R.'s originally. His father was a member of the convention that framed the present constitution of the state; he was, also, for some years chief justice of the state.

My master was never equal to his father, although he stood high at one time. He once lacked but a few votes of being elected Governor of the state: he once sat in the Assembly, and was generally a leading man in his own county. His influence was found to be greatest when exerted in favour of any measure in regard to the control of slaves. He was the first mover in several cruel and rigid municipal regulations in the county, which prohibited slaves from going over a certain number of miles from their master's places on the Sabbath, and from being seen about the town. He once instigated the authorities of the town where he attended service, to break up a Sabbath-school some humane members of the Methodist and Lutheran denominations had set up to teach the free negroes, lest the slaves should get some benefit of it.

But there was a still wider contrast between my master and his own children, eight in number, when I left him. His eldest daughter, the flower of the family, married a miserable and reckless gambler. His eldest son was kind-hearted, and rather a favourite with the slaves on that account; but he had no strength of mind or weight of character. His education was limited, and he had no disposition or tact for business of any kind. He died at thirty-six, intestate; leaving his second wife (a sister to his father's second wife) with several orphan children, a widow with a small estate deeply embarrassed. The second son was once sent to West Point to fit for an officer. After being there a short time, however, he became unsteady, and commenced the study of medicine, but he soon gave that up and preferred to live at home and flog the slaves; and by them was cordially dreaded and disliked, and among themselves he was vulgarly nicknamed on account of his cruel and filthy habits.

These two families will afford a fair illustration of the gloomy history of many others that I could name. This decline of slaveholding families is a subject of observation and daily remark among slaves; they are led to observe every change in the pecuniary, moral, and social state of the families they belong to, from the fact, that as the old master declines, or as his children are married off, they are expecting to fall into their hands, or in case of insolvency on the part of the old master, they expect to be sold; in either case, it involves a change of master--a subject to which they cannot be indifferent. And it is very rarely the case that a slave's condition is benefited by passing from the old master into the hands of one of his children. Owing to the causes I have mentioned, the decline is so rapid and marked, in almost every point of view, that the children of slaveholders are universally inferior to themselves, mentally, morally, physically, as well as pecuniarily, especially so in the latter point of view; and this is a matter of most vital concern to the slaves. The young master not being able to own as many slaves as his father, usually works what he has more severely, and being more liable to embarrassment, the slaves' liability to be sold at an early day is much greater. For the same reason, slaves have a deep interest, generally, in the marriage of a young mistress. Very generally the daughters of slaveholders marry inferior men; men who seek to better their own condition by a wealthy connection. The slaves who pass into the hands of the young master has had some chance to become acquainted with his character, bad as it may be; but the young mistress brings her slaves a new, and sometimes an unknown master. Sometimes these are the sons of already broken down slaveholders. In other cases they are adventurers from the north who remove to the south, and who readily become the most cruel masters.

APPENDIX.

These two letters are simply introduced to show what the state of my feelings was with reference to slavery at the time they were written. I had just heard several facts with regard to my parents, which had awakened my mind to great excitement.

TO MY FATHER, MOTHER, BROTHERS, AND SISTERS.

The following was written in **1844**:

DEARLY BELOVED IN BONDS,

About seventeen long years have now rolled away, since in the Providence of Almighty God, I left your embraces, and set out upon a daring adventure in search of freedom. Since that time, I have felt most severely the loss of the sun and moon and eleven stars from my social sky. Many, many a thick cloud of anguish has pressed my brow and sent deep down into my soul the bitter waters of sorrow in consequence. And you have doubtless had your troubles and anxious seasons also about your fugitive star.

I have learned that some of you have been sold, and again taken back by Colonel ----. How many of you are living and together, I cannot tell. My great grief is, lest you should have suffered this or some additional punishment on account of my *Exodus*.

I indulge the hope that it will afford you some consolation to know that your son and brother is yet alive. That God has dealt wonderfully and kindly with me in all my way. He has made me a Christian, and a Christian Minister, and thus I have drawn my support and comfort from that blessed Saviour, who came *to preach good tidings unto the meek, to bind up the broken hearted, to proclaim liberty to the captives; and the opening of the prison to them that are bound. To proclaim the acceptable year of the Lord and the day of vengeance of our God; to comfort all that mourn. To appoint unto them that mourn in Zion, to give unto them beauty for ashes, the oil of joy for mourning, the garment of praise for the spirit of heaviness, that they might be called trees of righteousness, the planting of the Lord that he might be glorified.*

If the course I took in leaving a condition which had become intolerable to me, has been made the occasion of making that condition worse to you in any way, I do most heartily regret such a change for the worse on your part. As I have no means, however, of knowing if such be the fact, so I have no means of making atonement, but by sincere prayer to Almighty God in your behalf, and also by taking this method of offering to you these consolations of the gospel to which I have just referred, and which I have found to be pre-eminently my own stay and support. My dear father and mother; I have very often wished, while administering the Holy Ordinance of Baptism to some scores of children brought forward by doting parents, that I could see you with yours among the number. And you, my brothers and sisters, while teaching hundreds of children and youths in schools over which I have been placed, what unspeakable delight I should have had in having you among the number; you may all judge of my feeling for these past years, when while preaching from Sabbath to Sabbath to congregations, I have not been so fortunate as even to see father, mother, brother, sister, uncle, aunt, nephew, niece, or cousin in my congregations. While visiting the sick, going to the house of mourning, and burying the dead, I have been a constant mourner for you. My sorrow has been that I know you are not in possession of those hallowed means of grace. I am thankful to you for those mild and gentle traits of character which you took such care to enforce upon me in my youthful days. As an evidence that I prize both you and them, I may say that at the age of thirty-seven, I find them as valuable as any lessons I have learned, nor am I ashamed to let it be known to the world, that I am the son of a bond man and a bond woman.

Let me urge upon you the fundamental truths of the Gospel of the Son of God. Let repentance towards God and faith in our Lord Jesus Christ have their perfect work in you, I beseech you. Do not be prejudiced against the gospel because it may be seemingly twisted into a support of slavery. The gospel rightly understood, taught, received, felt and practised, is anti-slavery as it is anti-sin. Just so far and so fast as the true spirit of the gospel obtains in the land, and especially in the lives of the oppressed, will the spirit of slavery sicken and become powerless like the serpent with his head pressed beneath the fresh leaves of the prickly ash of the forest.

There is not a solitary decree of the immaculate God that has been concerned in the ordination of slavery, nor does any possible development of his holy will sanctify it.

He has permitted us to be enslaved according to the invention of wicked men, instigated by the devil, with intention to bring good out of the evil, but He does not, He cannot approve of it. He has no need to approve of it, even on account of the good which He will bring out of it, for He could have brought about that very good in some other way.

God is never straitened; He is never at a loss for means to work. Could He not have made this a great and wealthy nation without making its riches to consist in our blood, bones, and souls? And could He not also have given the gospel to us without making us slaves?

My friends, let us then, in our afflictions, embrace and hold fast the gospel. The gospel is the fulness of God. We have the glorious and total weight of God's moral character in our side of the scale.

The wonderful purple stream which flowed for the healing of the nations, has a branch for us. Nay, is Christ divided? "The grace of God that bringeth salvation hath appeared to (for) all men, teaching us that denying ungodliness and worldly lust, we should live soberly, righteously, and godly in this present world, looking for that blessed hope and glorious appearing of the great God and our Saviour Jesus Christ, who gave himself for us that he might redeem us from all iniquity, and purify unto himself a peculiar people, zealous of good works."--Titus ii: 11-14.

But you say you have not the privilege of hearing of this gospel of which I speak. I know it; and this is my great grief. But you shall have it; I will send it to you by my humble prayer; I can do it; I will beg our heavenly Father, and he will preach this gospel to you in his holy providence.

You, dear father and mother cannot have much longer to live in this troublesome and oppressive world; you cannot bear the yoke much longer. And as you approach another world, how desirable it is

that you should have the prospect of a different destiny from what you have been called to endure in this world during a long life.

But it is the gospel that sets before you the hope of such a blessed rest as is spoken of in the word of God, Job iii. 17, 19. "There the wicked cease from troubling, and there the weary be at rest; there the prisoners rest together; they hear not the voice of the oppressors. The small and great are there; and the servant is free from his master."

Father, I know thy eyes are dim with age and weary with weeping, but look, dear father, yet a little while toward that haven. Look unto Jesus, "the author and finisher of thy faith," for the moment of thy happy deliverance is at hand.

Mother, dear mother, I know, I feel, mother, the pangs of thy bleeding heart, that thou hast endured, during so many years of vexation. Thy agonies are by a genuine son-like sympathy mine; I will, I must, I do share daily in those agonies of thine. But I sincerely hope that with me you bear your agonies to Christ who carries our sorrows.

O come then with me, my beloved family, of weary heart-broken and care-worn ones, to Jesus Christ, "casting all your care upon him, for he careth for you."--2 Peter v. 7.

With these words of earnest exhortation, joined with fervent prayer to God that He may smooth your rugged way, lighten your burden, and give a happy issue out of all your troubles, I must bid you adieu.

Your son and brother,

                JAS. P. *Alias* J. W. C. PENNINGTON.

The Fugitive Blacksmith

TO COLONEL F---- T----, OF H----, WASHINGTON COUNTY, MD. 1844.

DEAR SIR,

It is now, as you are aware, about seventeen years since I left your house and service, at the age of twenty. Up to that time, I was, according to your rule and claim, your slave. Till the age of seven years, I was, of course, of little or no service to you. At that age, however, you hired me out, and for three years I earned my support; at the age of ten years, you took me to your place again, and in a short time after you put me to work at the blacksmith's trade, at which, together with the carpentering trade, &c., I served you peaceably until the day I left you, with exception of the short time you had sold me to S---- H----, Esq., for seven hundred dollars. It is important for me to say to you, that I have no consciousness of having done you any wrong. I called you master when I was with you from the mere force of circumstances; but I never regarded you as my master. The nature which God gave me did not allow me to believe that you had any more right to me than I had to you, and that was just none at all. And from an early age, I had intentions to free myself from your claim. I never consulted any one about it; I had no advisers or instigators; I kept my own counsel entirely concealed in my own bosom. I never meditated any evil to your person or property, but I regarded you as my oppressor, and I deemed it my duty to get out of your hands by peaceable means.

I was always obedient to your commands. I laboured for you diligently at all times. I acted with fidelity in any matter which you entrusted me. As you sometimes saw fit to entrust me with considerable money, to buy tools or materials, not a cent was ever coveted or kept.

During the time I served you in the capacity of blacksmith, your materials were used economically, your work was done expeditiously, and in the very best style, a style second to no smith in your neighbourhood. In short, sir, you well know that my habits from early life were advantageous to you. Drinking, gambling, fighting, &c., were not my habits. On Sabbaths, holidays, &c., I was frequently at your service, when not even your body-servant was at home.

Times and times again, I have gone on Sunday afternoon to H----, six miles, after your letters and papers, when it was as much my privilege to be *"out of the way,"* as it was C----.

But what treatment did you see fit to return me for all this? You, in the most unfeeling manner, abused my father for no cause but speaking a word to you, as a man would speak to his fellow-man, for the sake simply of a better understanding.

You vexed my mother, and because she, as a tender mother would do, showed solicitude for the virtue of her daughters, you threatened her in an insulting brutal manner.

You abused my brother and sister without cause, and in like manner you did to myself; you surmised evil against me. You struck me with your walking-cane, called me insulting names, threatened me, swore at me, and became more and more wrathy in your conduct, and at the time I quitted your place, I had good reason to believe that you were meditating serious evil against me.

Since I have been out of your hands, I have been signally favoured of God, whence I infer that in leaving you, I acted strictly in accordance with his holy will. I have a conscience void of offence towards God and towards all men, yourself not excepted. And I verily believe that I have performed a sacred duty to God and myself, and a kindness to you, in taking the blood of my soul peaceably off your soul. And now, dear sir, having spoken somewhat pointedly, I would, to convince you of my perfect good will towards you, in the most kind and respectful terms, remind you of your coming destiny. You are now over seventy years of age, pressing on to eternity with the weight of these seventy years upon you. Is not this enough without the blood of some half-score of souls?

You are aware that your right to property in man is now disputed by the civilized world. You are fully aware, also, that the question, whether the Bible sanctions slavery, has distinctly divided this nation in sentiment. On the side of Biblical Anti slavery, we have many of the most learned, wise and holy men in the land. If the Bible affords no sanction to slavery, (and I claim that it cannot,) then it must be a sin of the deepest dye; and can you, sir, think to go to God in hope with a sin of such magnitude upon your soul?

But admitting that the question is yet doubtful, (which I do only for the sake of argument,) still, sir, you will have the critical hazard of this doubt pressing, in no very doubtful way, upon your declining years, as you descend the long and tedious hill of life.

Would it not seem to be exceedingly undesirable to close an eventful probation of seventy or eighty years, and leave your reputation among posterity suspended upon so doubtful an issue? But what, my dear sir, is a reputation among posterity, who are but worms, compared with a destiny in the world of spirits? And it is in light of that destiny that I would now have you look at this subject. You and I, and all that you claim as your slaves, are in a state of probation; our great business is to serve God under His righteous moral government. Master and slave are the subjects of that government, bound by its immutable requirements, and liable to its sanctions in the next world, though enjoying its forbearance in this. You will pardon me then for pressing this point in earnest good faith. You should, at this stage, review your life without political bias, or adherence to long cherished prejudices, and remember that you are soon to meet those whom you have held, and do hold in slavery, at the awful bar of the impartial Judge of all who doeth right. Then what will become of your own doubtful claims? What will be done with those doubts that agitated your mind years ago; will you answer for threatening, swearing, and using the cowhide among your slaves?

What will become of those long groans and unsatisfied complaints of your slaves, for vexing them with insulting words, placing them in the power of dogish and abusive overseers, or under your stripling, misguided, hot-headed son, to drive and whip at pleasure, and for selling parts or whole families to Georgia? They will all meet you at that bar. Uncle James True, Charles Cooper, Aunt Jenny, and the native Africans; Jeremiah, London, and Donmore, have already gone a-head, and only wait your arrival--Sir, I shall meet you there. The account between us for the first twenty years of my life, will have a definite

character upon which one or the other will be able to make out a case.

Upon such a review as this, sir, you will, I am quite sure, see the need of seriousness. I assure you that the thought of meeting you in eternity, and before the dread tribunal of God, with a complaint in my mouth against you, is to me of most weighty and solemn character. And you will see that the circumstances from which this thought arises are of equal moment to yourself. Can the pride of leaving your children possessed of long slave states, or the policy of sustaining in the state the institution of slavery, justify you in overlooking a point of moment to your future happiness?

What excuse could you offer at the bar of God, favoured as you have been with the benefits of a refined education, and through a long life with the gospel of love, should you, when arraigned there, find that you have, all your life long, laboured under a great mistake in regard to slavery, and that in this mistake you had died, and only lifted up your eyes in the light of eternity to be corrected, when it was too late to be corrected in any other way.

I could wish to address you (being bread, born, and raised in your family) *as a father in Israel, or as an elder brother in Christ, but I cannot; mockery is a sin.* I can only say then, dear sir, farewell, till I meet you at the bar of God, where Jesus, who died for us, will judge between us. Now his blood can wash out our stain, break down the middle wall of partition, and reconcile us not only to God but to each other, then the word of his mouth, the sentence will set us at one. As for myself, I am quite ready to meet you face to face at the bar of God. I have done you no

wrong; I have nothing to fear when we both fall into the hands of the just God.

I beseech you, dear sir, to look well and consider this matter soundly. In yonder world you can have no slaves--you can be no man's master--you can neither sell, buy, or whip, or drive. Are you then, by sustaining the relation of a slaveholder, forming a character to dwell with God in peace?

With kind regards,
I am, sir, yours respectfully,

                                                            J. W. C. PENNINGTON.

LIBERTY'S CHAMPION.

BY A FRIEND OF THE AUTHOR'S.

ON the wings of the wind he comes, he comes!
With the rolling billow's speed;
On his breast are the signs of peace and love,
And his soul is nerved with strength from above:
While his eyes flash fire,
He burns with desire
To achieve the noble deed.

To the shores of the free he goes, he goes!
And smiles as he passes on;
He hears the glad notes of Liberty's song,
And bids the brave sons of freedom be strong.
While his heart bounds high
To his crown in the sky,
He triumphs o'er conquests won.

To the homes of the slave he flies, he flies!
Where manacled mourners cry;
The bursting groan of the mind's o'erflow,
Transfixed on the dark and speaking brow:
With a murmuring sound,

Ascends from the ground,
To the God that reigns on high.

To his loved Father's throne he hastes, he hastes!
And pours forth his soul in grief:
Uprising he finds his strength renewed,
And his heart with fervent love is imbued;
While the heaving sigh,
And the deep-toned cry,
Appeal for instant relief.

To the hard oppressor he cries, he cries,
And points to the bleeding slave;
He tells of the rights of the human soul,
And his eyes with full indignation roll:
While his heart is moved,
And the truth is proved,
He seeks the captive to save.

Again to the foeman he speaks, he speaks,
But utters his cry in vain;
He breathes no curse, no vengeance seeks,--
For the broken hearts or the anguished shrieks,
For the mother's pains,
Or the father's gains,--
Upon the oppressor's name.

To nations of freemen once more he comes,
To raise Liberty's banner high;
He tells of the wrongs of the bonded slave,

And cries aloud, 'mid throngs of the brave,
"O freemen, arise!
Be faithful and wise,
And answer the mourner's cry.

In melting strains of love he calls, he calls,
To the great and good from afar;
Till sympathy wakes to the truthful tale,
And the prayer of the faith, which cannot fail,
Ascends to heaven,
And grace is given,
To nerve for the bloodless war.

The truth with a magic power prevails:
All hearts are moved to the strife;
In a holy phalanx, and with deathless aim,
They seek a peaceful triumph to gain
O'er the tyrant's sway,
In his onward way,
To raise the fallen to life.

At the mighty voice of the glorious free
The chain of the oppressor breaks;
The slave from his bondage springs forth to love,
And, standing erect, his eye fixed above,
He honours his race,
And in the world's face,
The language of liberty speaks.

The oppressor no longer owns a right,

>   Or property claims in the slave,
>   But the world, in the glory of freedom's
> light,
>   Beams out from the darkness of wide-
> spread night;
>   Throughout its length,
>   In greatness and strength,
>   The honour of the free and brave. Printed for CHARLES GILPIN, 5, Bishopgate Street Without.

The Fugitive Blacksmith, or Events in the History of JAMES W. C. PENNINGTON, Pastor of a Presbyterian Church, New York. Foolscap 8vo., sewed, price 1s.

"This entrancing narrative * * * We trust that thousands of our readers will procure the volume, which is published by Mr. Gilpin at a mere trifle--much too cheap to accomplish the purpose for which, in part or mainly, it has been published--the raising a fund to remove the pecuniary burdens which press on the author's flock. NOTHING SHORT OF THE SALE OF FIFTY THOUSAND or SIXTY THOUSAND COPIES could be at all availing for this object. * * * We very cordially recommend him and his narrative to the kind consideration of our readers. Let them load him with English hospitality, fill his purse, and send him back as fast as possible to the land of his early bondage, of his matured freedom, and to the people to whose character and capabilities he does so much honour."--*Christian Witness,* October, 1849.

"The principal portion of the 'Tract,' as Mr. Pennington modestly styles his book, consists of an autobiography of his early life as a slave, and of his escape from bondage, and final settlement in New York as a Presbyterian Minister. His adventures and hair-breadth escapes invest the narrative with startling interest, and excite the deepest sympathies of the reader."--*Nonconformist,* September, 26th, 1849.

"Believing that by the purchase of this little book our readers will confer a benefit on the writer, at the same time that they become possessed of a narrative of deep interest, we give it our most cordial recommendation."--*Teetotal Times,* October, 1849.

London: CHARLES GILPIN, 5, Bishopsgate Street Without.

CHARLES GILPIN'S LIST OF NEW BOOKS, 5, BISHOPSGATE STREET WITHOUT.

The Acknowledged Doctrines of the Church of Rome. Being an Exposition of Roman Catholic Doctrines, as set forth by esteemed doctors of the said Church, and confirmed by repeated publication, with the sanction of Bishops and Ministers of her Religion. By SAMUEL CAPPER: 8vo. cloth, lettered, price 14s.

The Island of Cuba: its Resources, Progress and Prospects, considered especially in relation to the influence of its prosperity on the interests of the British West India Colonies. By R. R. MADDEN, M. R. I. A. 12mo., cloth, price 3s. 6d.

"This little volume contains a large amount of valuable information, intimately connected with the progress of society and happiness of man."--*Christian Times.*

"We recommend the book to the perusal of all who are interested in the great work of negro emancipation."--*Standard of Freedom.*

"As supplying the latest information concerning Cuba, Mr. Madden's book is extremely valuable."--*Economist.*

"We cordially recommend the volume."--*Anti-Slavery Reporter.*

A Voyage to the Slave Coasts of West and East Africa. By the Rev. PASOO [illegible] GRENFELL HILL, R.N., Author of "Fifty Days on Board a Slave Vessel." 12mo., cloth, lettered, price 1s.

"This brief but interesting narrative proceeds from one who has witnessed the horrors of the Slave-trade, as carried on in various parts of the globe. * * * * The unpretending style in which the narrative is written, and the stamp of truth which it carries with it, induce us to recommend it to an extensive perusal."--*Standard of Freedom.*

The Fugitive Blacksmith; or Events in the History of JAMES W. C. PENNINGTON, Pastor of a Presbyterian Church, New York. Foolscap 8vo., sewed. The sixth thousand. price 1s.

"This entrancing narrative * * * We trust that thousands of our readers will procure the volume, which is published by Mr. Gilpin at a mere trifle--much too cheap to accomplish the purpose for which, in part or mainly, it has been published--the raising a fund to remove the pecuniary burdens which press on the author's flock. NOTHING SHORT OF THE SALE OF FIFTY THOUSAND or SIXTY THOUSAND COPIES could be at all availing for this object. * * * We very cordially recommend him and his narrative to the kind consideration of our readers"--*Christian Witness.*

Sparks from the Anvil. By ELIHU BURRITT. 12mo., sewed. The thirteenth thousand, price 1s.

"These are Sparks indeed of singular brilliancy."--*British Friend.*

"They deserve to be stereotyped, and to form part of the standard literature of the age."--*Kentish Independent.*

"We say to all, read it, imbibe its spirit, and learn, like the writer, to work for and with God, towards the regeneration of your race."--*Nottingham Review.*

"Reader, if you have not read the 'Sparks from the Anvil,' do so at once."--*The Echo.*

A Voice from the Forge. By ELIHU BURRITT, with a Portrait. Being a sequel to "Sparks from the Anvil." 12mo., sewed, price 1s.

"In every line coined from the reflecting mind of the Blacksmith of Massachusetts, there is a high philosophy and philanthropy genuine and pure. His sympathies are universal, his aspirations are for the happiness of all, and his writings are nervous, terse, and vigorous."--*London Telegraph.*

"The influence of the small work before us must be for good, and we wish it every success. The various essays it contains are written with natural eloquence, and contain many just and original sentiments."--*Scottish Press.*

The Prize Essay on Juvenile Depravity. By the Rev. H. WORSLEY, A.M., Easton Rectory, Suffolk, To this Essay on Juvenile Depravity, as connected with the causes and practices of Intemperance, and the effectual barrier opposed by them to education, the above Prize of £100. was awarded by the Adjudicators, Dr. Harris of Cheshunt; the Rev. James Sherman, Surrey Chapel; and Dr. Vaughan of Harrow. Post 8vo., cloth, price 5s.

"We earnestly commend this very able essay to the early attention of those whose philanthropy leads them to seek a remedy for the fearful amount of juvenile depravity which now gangrenes society, and will prove fatal if not checked and removed. The author admirably uses his statistics, and shows an intimate knowledge of human nature, in its multifarious circumstances."--*Christian Examiner,* April, 1849.

"It is impossible to read many sentences of this volume without perceiving that you are in the company of a Christian philanthropist--a man who is bent, as far as in him lies, on the removal of a great national evil; and who has sufficient patience and courage to investigate the sources of that evil, to examine with candour the various remedies proposed for its removal, and to point out with honesty that which he believes to be the only appropriate and effectual remedy. We might say much in praise of the *style* in which the essay is written,--it is elegant, classical, and pointed,--but we choose rather to dwell on the importance of the matter."--*Teetotal Times,* April, 1849.

"We may observe that this Prize Essay, as a whole, will amply repay a perusal; the statistics it contains are especially valuable and instructive. We strongly recommend our friends to obtain the work, and read it for themselves."--*The British Friend,* March, 1849.

"Mr. Worsley's is unquestionably a very able treatise."--*Patriot,* April, 1849.

An Inquiry into the Extent and Causes of Juvenile Depravity. Dedicated, by special permission, to the Right Hon. the Earl of Carlisle. By THOMAS BEGGS, late Secretary of the Health of Towns' Association, and author of "Lectures on the Moral Elevation of the People." 8vo., cloth, price 5s.

"Few men were better qualified to deal with such a case than Mr. Beggs, whose lot it has been largely to be mixed up with the working classes, and who has made their characters, habits, and circumstances, the subject of his special study. He is, moreover, a man of strong penetrating intellect, and possesses in a high degree whatever is needful to constitute a student of human nature. Let all read Mr. Beggs's volume. A heart brought very largely into sympathy with the subject could scarcely read a chapter of it without tears. Its revelations are those of the darkest chambers of spiritual death and moral desolation. The work has our cordial commendation. It is one of the class of books which cannot be too widely circulated."--*British Banner,* August 25th, 1849.

"Mr. Beggs writes with all the confidence which a practical knowledge of the subject has given him, and it is impossible to peruse the pages of his work without obtaining a fearful insight into the extent of the moral depravity of the lower orders of society. In the paths of vice in which his reverend competitor fears to tread, there Mr. Beggs boldly steps forward, and denounces while he exposes those gigantic and appalling evils, which must be brought to light before they can be effectually grappled with and overcome."--*Journal of Public Health,* July, 1849.

"Whether we regard the graphic picture of the actual condition of the neglected classes, or the important collection of original and selected statistics which this volume contains, we must pronounce it to be one of the most trustworthy expositions of our social state and evils which has yet been produced."--*Truth Seeker,* July, 1849.

Sand and Canvass: a Narrative of Adventures in Egypt, with a Sojourn among the Artists in Rome, &c. With Illustrations. By SAMUEL BEVAN. 8vo., cloth, price 12s.

"The random high spirits of this book give *salt* to the sand, and *colour* to the canvass."--*Athenæum.*

"The truth is never disguised, but things are mentioned with an air of sincerity that is irresistible. We never recollect to have opened a book which possessed this charm in anything approaching to the name degree. It captivates and excites, giving reality and interest to every incident that is introduced."--*Morning Post.*

Fifty days on Board a Slave Vessel. By the Rev. PASOO [illegible] GRENFELL HILL, M.A., Chaplain of H. M. S. Cleopatra. Demy 12mo., cloth, lettered, price 1s. 6d.

"This curious and succinct narrative gives the experience of a short voyage on board one of the slave ships. We shall be rejoiced, if the publicity given to this little but intelligent work by our means, assist in drawing the attention of the influential classes to the subject."--*Blackwood's Magazine.*

"We hope this little work will have a wide circulation. We can conceive nothing so likely to do good to the subject cause it is intended to promote."--*Examiner.*

"Mr. Hill is a pleasant, unaffected, and elegant writer, with a fund of good sense, and his brief and popular work is well adapted for general circulation."--*Spectator.*

Captain Sword and Captain Pen; A Poem. By LEIGH HUNT. Third Edition. With a New Preface, Remarks on War, and Notes detailing the Horrors on which the Poem is founded. Foolscap 8vo., cloth, gilt edges, price 3s. 6d.

The Pastor's Wife. A Memoir of Mrs. Sherman, of Surrey Chapel. By her Husband. Second Edition, with a Portrait, foolscap 8vo., cloth, price 5s..

"This constitutes one of the most tender, beautiful, instructive, and edifying narratives that for a long time has come under our notice. * * * We anticipate for it a very extended popularity and usefulness among the mothers and daughters of England."--*Christian Witness,* January, 1849.

"We have been truly delighted and instructed by the perusal of this Memoir. It is fresh and beautiful in the display of all the practical graces of the Christian character. It will be a blessing and a consolation, we doubt not, to hundreds of Christians. From its authorship we are delighted to think it will obtain a wide circulation."--*Evangelical Magazine,* January, 1849.

"This excellent book will, doubtless, attain a high place in our religious literature. We have read nothing half so touching as the account given of the closing scene of Mrs. Sherman's earthly career."--*Court Journal,* September 8th, 1849.

"This volume deserves a wide circulation. However painful the task Mr. Sherman undertook in compiling the Memoir, we are persuaded he will be repaid by the benefit it will confer upon the members of the Church of Christ."--*Wesleyan Times,* January 23rd, 1849.

"This volume deserves a large circulation, and we feel it a pleasure to commend its perusal to the various classes of our readers, especially to those whose sex may enable them to tread in Mrs. Sherman's steps."--*Nonconformist,* January 24th, 1849.

The Demerara Martyr. Memoirs of the Rev. JOHN SMITH. Missionary to Demerara. By EDWIN ANGEL WALLBRIDGE. With a Preface by the Rev. W. G. BARRETT. 8vo., cloth, price 7s.

"There will one day be a resurrection of names and reputations, as certainly as of bodies."--*John Milton.*

"The book is a worthy monument to the distinguished Martyr whose history forms its leading subject. * * * A valuable contribution to the cause of freedom, humanity, and justice in Demerara."--*Patriot.*

"We have perused this work with mixed feelings of pain and admiration; pain, arising from the sense of wrong and misery inflicted on a good man; admiration, that the author has so fully redeemed his friend and brother minister from calumnies and misrepresentations of Satanic malice and wickedness."--*Standard of Freedom,* August 30th, 1848.

"A work of great interest by one of the Missionary labourers has just appeared, under the title of the 'Martyr of Demerara.' It consists of Memoirs of the Rev. John Smith, Missionary of that colony in the times of rampant slavery; and details the events in the history of that devoted and persecuted man, which closed in his virtual martyrdom--an event which never ceased to influence the public mind in England until colonial slavery itself had ceased to be."--*Leeds Mercury,* September 10th, 1849.

A Popular Life of George Fox, the First of the Quakers; compiled from his Journal and other authentic sources, and interspersed with remarks on the imperfect reformation of the Anglican Church, and the consequent spread of dissent. By JOSIAH MARSH. 8vo., cloth, price 6s. 6d.

The work abounds with remarkable incidents, which pourtray a vivid picture of the excited feelings that predominated during those eventful periods of our history-- the Commonwealth and the Restoration.

The Campaner Thal: Or, Discourses on the Immortality of the Soul. Foolscap 8vo., price 2s 6d. By JEAN PAUL FR. RICHTER. Translated from the German by JULIETTE BAUKR.

"-- Report, we regret to say, is all that we know of the 'Campaner Thal,' one of Richter's beloved topics, or rather the life of his whole philosophy, glimpses of which look forth on us from almost every one of his writings. He died while engaged, under recent and almost total blindness, in enlarging and remodelling this 'Campaner Thal.' The unfinished manuscript was borne upon his coffin to the burial vault; and Klopstock's hymn, 'Auferstehen wirst du!' 'Thou shalt arise my soul,' can seldom have been sung with more appropriate application than over the grave of Jean Paul."--From *Carlyle's Miscellanies.*

A Kiss for a Blow. (Twenty-third thousand.) A Collection of Stories for Children, showing them how to prevent quarrelling. By H. C. WRIGHT. In 18mo., price 1s.

"Of this little book it is impossible to speak too highly--it is the reflex of the spirit of childhood, full of tenderness, pity, and love: quick to recent, and equally quick to forgive. We wish that all children could imbibe its spirit, then indeed would the world be happier and better."--*Mary Howitt.*

"This volume, of which it were to be wished that every family in the country had a copy, has been reprinted in London by Charles Gilpin; it is an invaluable little book."--*Chambers's Tracts.*

Portraits in Miniature, or Sketches of Character in Verse. By HENRIETTA J. FRY, Author of the "Hymns of the Reformation," &c. Illustrated with Eight Engravings. 8vo., price 10s. 6d. This little volume holds many a name dear to the best interests of society, like those of Elizabeth Fry, J. J. Gurney, W. Wilberforce, Hannah More, Bishop Heber, &c.; and it is thought that such a transcript of those who have as it were trodden the paths of life by our side, may serve to quicken amongst us, the fragrance of their Christian graces, and like living Epistles written on our hearts speak to our spirits the language "Come up hither."

A Selection of Scripture Poetry. By LOVELL SQUIRE. Third Edition, containing many original Hymns not hitherto published. 18mo., cloth, price 2s. 6d. The same to be had nicely bound in silk, with gilt edges, price 4s.

The Autobiography of a Working Man, by "One WHO MAN WHISTLED AT THE PLOUGH." This work contains the "Barrack Life of a Drageon;" what the author did to save Britain from a Revolution; his Court Martial and Punishment at Birmingham; the Conspiracy of the Secret Committee of the Trade Unions in London to "Assassinate the Cabinet Ministers, and Capture the Palace, Royal Family, and Bank of England;" how planned and how prevented. Post 8vo., cloth, price 7s.

"Here is a genuine, fresh, and thoroughly true book; something really worth reading and remembering."--*Manchester Examiner.*

"The well-known author of this work, who has attracted much public attention, and has acquired a well merited reputation, has done the public a great service by publishing his autobiography."--*Economist.*

"This is one of the most interesting works which has come under our notice for a long time. It is the genuine record of the inner and outer life of a genuine working man. * * * There are few writings in our language, which, for power of graphic description, surpass the letters by him under the signature of 'One who has Whistled at the Plough;' and in his autobiography we find the same facility of description, &c."--*Leeds Times.*

The Rhyming Game; a Historiette. 16mo., sewed, price 6d.

This little book is designed as a winter evening recreation for young persons. Its object is, that of calling up their ideas into ready exercise, and habituating the mind to a prompt and accurate description of object, as well as a more subtle delineation of thoughts and feelings; and it has particularly in view the monition that, even in their recreations, they may remember "l'utile," as well as "l'agreeable."

Skyrack; a Fairy Tale. With Six Illustrations. Post 8vo., cloth extra, price 2s. 6d.

"It is simply the story of an old oak; but it carries you away to the forest, and refreshes you with its dewy, sunny, solitary life. The spirit of the book is pure as the breezes of the forest themselves. All the imagery, and the whole tone of the story are of that kind which you wish to pervade the mind of your children. In a word, we have rarely enjoyed a more delicious hour, or have been more thoroughly wrapt in sweet, silent, dewy, and balmy forest entrancement, than during the perusal of Skyrack."--*Standard of Freedom.*

The Pastor's Legacy; or, Devotional Fragments. From the German of Lavater. By HENRIETTA J. FRY. 18mo., silk, price 2s. 6d.

"This is an exquisite little gem."--*Christian Examiner.*

** An edition may be obtained with the German appended to the work, done up in the same manner, for 3s.

The Peasantry of England; an Appeal on behalf of the Working Classes; in which the causes which have led to their present impoverished and degraded condition, and the means by which it may best be permanently improved, are clearly pointed out. By G. M. Perry. 12mo., cloth, price 4s.

Dymond's Essays on the Principles of Morality, and on the Private and Political Rights and Obligations of Mankind. Royal 8vo., paper cover. 3s. 6d. Neat embossed cloth, 4s. 6d.

The high standard of morality to which these Essays aim at directing the attention of mankind, justly entitle them to the extensive circulation which they have obtained in three previous editions; and the present cheap and popular form in which they now appear, having reached a sale of nearly Seven Thousand in twelve months, is an unequivocal proof of public approbation.

Cards of Character: a Biographical Game. In a neat case, price 5s.

"This game contains much amusement and instruction. It consists of brief sketches of the lives and characters of about seventy of the principal persons of the past age, and questions corresponding in number with the Cards. The game is well arranged, and very simple."

Hymns of the Reformation. By Luther and others. from the German; to which is added his Life from the original Latin of Melancthon, by the Author of "The Pastor's Legacy." 18mo, neatly bound in silk, 3s. 6d.

An Encyclopædia of Facts, Anecdotes, Arguments, and Illustrations from History, Philosophy, and Christianity, in support of the principles of Permanent and Universal Peace. BY EDWIN PAXTON HOOD, Author of "Fragments of Thought and Composition," &c. 18mo., sewed, price 1s. 6d.

Parables: translated from the German of Krumacher. Containing the Hyacinth; the Persian, the Jew and the Christian; Asaph and Heman; Life and Death; the Mother's Faith, &c. 16mo., sewed, price 1s.

Memoirs of Paul Cuffee, a Man of Colour. Compiled from authentic sources. By WILSON ARMISTEAD. 18mo., cloth, price 1s.

"The exertions of this truly benevolent individual entitles him to the esteem of the world, and the grateful remembrance of latest posterity."

How Little Henry of Eichenfels came to the Knowledge of God. 16mo., sewed, price 1s.

Ireland's Welcome to the Stranger; or Excursions through Ireland in 1844 and 1845, for the purpose of personally investigating the condition of the poor. By A. NICHOLSON of New York. 12mo., cloth, price 5s.

"We have derived much pleasure from Miss Nicholson's book--it is worth a cart-load of such absurd books as Kohl's, which, brimful of blunders, was nevertheless much praised and widely circulated."--*Tait's Magazine.*

Narrative of a Recent Journey of Six Weeks in Ireland, in connexion with the subject of supplying small seed to some of the remoter districts; with current observations on the depressed circumstances of the people, and the means presented for the permanent improvement of their social condition. By WILLIAM BENNETT. 12mo., cloth, price 2s.

"Nor will I give the slightest countenance to any consideration of Ireland, as a thing separate and apart from ourselves."--*Old MS.*

"We cordially recommend 'Six Weeks in Ireland,' by W. Bennett; the work is cheap--full of daguerreotype drawings from life--not of course, ordinary drawings, but plain pen-and-ink sketches; by which one may comprehend the whole matter that came under the writer's notice."--*Tait's Magazine.*

The Water Cure. Letters from Grafenberg in the years 1843-4-5, and 6. By JOHN GIBBS. 12mo., cloth, price 4s. 6d.

"The inquirers after health, the philanthropist, and the medical practitioner will do well to read Mr. Gibbs' book, for which we thank him, and which we beg very sincerely to recommend to careful perusal."--*Nonconformist.* September 8th, 1849.

"We strongly recommend its perusal."--*Limerick Chronicle Chronicle.*

The Water Cure. Cases of Disease cured by Cold Water, translated from the German, with physiological illustrations from orthodox medical authors. By K. S. ABDY, M.A. Second Edition, 8vo., sewed, price 4s. 6d.

Defensive War proved to be a Denial of Christianity, and of the Government of God. With Illustrative Facts and Anecdotes. By H. C. WRIGHT. Price 2s.

CHARLES GILPIN, 5, Bishopsgate Street Without.

Made in the USA
Monee, IL
22 August 2020